Start UNSELLING NOW

Rajesh Grover is a renowned sales strategist with over two decades of experience in evolving sales strategies to meet changing market demands. His expertise in integrating technology enhances sales methods, giving teams a competitive edge and setting them ahead in the industry.

Grover's approach masterfully blends theory with practice, simplifying complex concepts to make them accessible and actionable for sales professionals across various sectors. This clarity allows teams to swiftly adapt and implement these strategies, driving measurable and enduring results.

Known for his innovative tactics and deep market insights, Rajesh has a proven track record of transforming sales functions into high-performing teams. As a sought-after sales coach, his methods not only boost performance but also cultivate lasting customer relationships and loyalty, establishing him as a key influencer in the sales community.

Start UNSELLING NOW

The Sales **MANIFESTO** for Winning Customers

RAJESH GROVER

Published by
Rupa Publications India Pvt. Ltd 2024
7/16, Ansari Road, Daryaganj
New Delhi 110002

Sales centres:
Bengaluru Chennai
Hyderabad Jaipur Kathmandu
Kolkata Mumbai Prayagraj

Copyright © Rajesh Grover 2024

The views and opinions expressed in this book are the author's own and the facts are as reported by him, which have been verified to the extent possible, and the publishers are not in any way liable for the same.

All rights reserved.

No part of this publication may be reproduced, transmitted, or stored in a retrieval system, in any form or by any means, electronic, mechanical, photocopying, recording or otherwise, without the prior permission of the publisher.

P-ISBN: 978-93-6156-825-1
E-ISBN: 978-93-6156-075-0

First impression 2024

10 9 8 7 6 5 4 3 2 1

The moral right of the author has been asserted.

Printed in India

This book is sold subject to the condition that it shall not, by way of trade or otherwise, be lent, resold, hired out, or otherwise circulated, without the publisher's prior consent, in any form of binding or cover other than that in which it is published.

With deepest gratitude, I dedicate this book to:

Almighty God, for the wisdom and grace that has made this endeavour possible.
My parents, for their unconditional support, love, and the values that have shaped my life.
And my wife, for her love, patience and constant encouragement, which has been my source of strength and inspiration.

Contents

Foreword — *ix*
Introduction — *xiii*

1. You, Your and Yourself — 1
2. Your Customer — 26
3. Your Product and Service — 51
4. Your Playbook — 60
5. Master Your Openings — 77
6. Your Customer Profiling and Value Proposition — 90
7. Objections—Your Friend or Foe — 105
8. Making Objections Your Best Friend — 117
9. Sharpen Your Closing Skills — 150
10. Your Customer Service — 191
11. Your Referrals — 200
12. Technology—Your Unfair Advantage — 210
13. Parting Notes — 225

Acknowledgements — 228

Foreword

Ten years ago, I embarked on a journey to visit our operational businesses across Southeast Asia. I spent four weeks on the road, meeting our local managing directors in the region. When I arrived in the mega city of Dhaka late at night, it was both hot and humid. Jetlagged and excited, with only a few hours of sleep, I found myself in our Dhaka office the next morning, where I met Rajesh—whom I fondly call Raj—for the first time in person.

Raj and I had spoken frequently before—mostly about finance, marketing and HR matters. Our conversations were always focused and structured, but even then, there was an undeniable sense of trust between us. It was clear from our first interaction that Raj had a unique approach to sales. His focus wasn't just on closing deals—it was on understanding the customer deeply. Raj had this incredible knack for seeing the world through the customer's eyes, prioritizing their needs, and making them feel like they were part of the process rather than just being sold to.

Back then, Bangladesh's internet penetration was only 12%, and in a country of 160 million people, transacting real estate online seemed like an impossible task. But Raj wasn't fazed. While many stuck to Western sales methods that often fell short in emerging markets, Raj thrived on finding solutions that truly worked for his customers. He developed an SMS sales solution, an old-school technology in a modern world but perfect for a market with limited internet access. His out-of-the-box thinking allowed him to turn what seemed unsellable into a success, not by force-selling, but by creating an environment where the customer chose to buy. The result: complete turnaround of the business.

That first day, we spent hours discussing business strategies, marketing plans, and how to tackle a market like Bangladesh. By the end of the day, I wasn't in the mood for a big dinner or drinks, but Raj, ever observant, surprised me with local food and a bottle of gin and tonic. That night, we left business behind and shared stories from our lives. I learned that Raj's journey had taken him from a tech geek to sales mastermind. Whether in FMCG, alcobev, luxury, real estate, retail, food and beverage or e-commerce, his success came from one guiding principle: always putting the customer first.

By the end of that night in Dhaka, with the food eaten and drinks finished, we found ourselves talking about what truly mattered—our families, cultures and beliefs. That night laid the foundation for a lifelong friendship, and now, with this book, Raj is sharing the wisdom that has made him one of the most successful salespeople I've ever known.

Raj's method of prioritizing the customer is what made him so successful in some of the toughest markets around the world. It's not just about selling—it's about helping the customer see the value for themselves. This ability to 'unsell' has been the driving force behind Raj's business turnarounds in the most challenging conditions. Regardless of the country or market, or the industry or sector, Raj has always found a way to adapt his approach to different products, markets, and circumstances. Time and time again, he took what others thought was unsellable and transformed it into something the customer wanted to buy.

In *Start Unselling Now*, Raj doesn't just share his experiences. He teaches the same methodologies he has used to train thousands of successful salespeople across the globe. Every lesson in this book is grounded in Raj's belief that the best salespeople don't just sell—they create environments where customers feel empowered to make decisions on their own. Raj's structured, customer-first approach has become a blueprint for sales teams around the world, proving that you don't need to hard-sell to succeed. By understanding your customer deeply and truly prioritizing their needs, the 'unsellable' becomes a natural purchase.

Whether you're an experienced salesperson or just starting out, I have no doubt you'll find the insights in this book invaluable in your journey.

Yours,
Mo

Muhammad Said Chahrour
Managing Director of GGW Insurance Group

Introduction

Selling is hard! It's a phrase echoed by many salespeople that I have encountered for over two decades of working in sales. Initially, like many, I dismissed this notion. After all, I witnessed top salespeople reaping abundant rewards and success.

However, as I traversed the world of sales, from mass-market commodities to luxury goods, training and coaching thousands of salespeople across diverse industries and continents, I came to the realization that 'selling is indeed hard'. This is even more true in today's ever-changing and dynamic world with diverse customer segments, increasing cost of customer acquisition and fierce competition.

In today's era of the modern buyer, traditional sales tactics, as we once knew them, have become obsolete. Gone are the days of pushy pitches and aggressive persuasion. The game has evolved, and rules have changed. Success today demands a different approach. In the last decade and a half, there has been a significant evolution in the buyers' landscape. We have seen the entry and rise of Generation Z (and now Generation Alpha) into the customer set, how AI and technology are disrupting industries, and how salespeople, sitting in one corner of the world, are handling customers on the other side of the world. This image is the true globalization of the markets and the customer base.

This evolution has not only reshaped the buyer's landscape but also redefined the essence of sales itself. The modern buyer is well-informed and digitally savvy. Their buying journey is no longer linear, but a complex web of touch points across various channels, both online and offline. They demand authenticity, transparency and personalization, valuing experiences and relationships over mere transactions. To handle the buyer of today with the old selling tactics is like trying to shoot a target with your eyes closed, and we all know what happens when you do that.

So, the golden question is: if selling is hard, then how does one make a successful career in sales? The answer came through reflection and through the experience of dealing with thousands of customers from all over the world. Slicing and dicing every root cause of a successful outcome vs. an unsuccessful one, pointed to one incontrovertible truth: **selling to customers does not work!**

It's human psychology. Anyone who is paying for a product or a service wants to feel that they made that decision and not that someone sold it to them. Because at the end of the deal, the customer wants to feel they are the 'king' and the salesperson acted as the best advisor to help them make the decision. Think about it: as a consumer, do you prefer feeling manipulated into a purchase, or empowered to make a choice? The answer is evident.

The modern buyer has heralded a big change to what we have known about customers. The big change is: it isn't about how you want to sell anymore, but rather it is about how the customer wants to buy. What does this mean in layman's terms? It is no more about **just** the right product, the right price, the right placement or the right time. Rather, it is **also** about the seamless buying journey, personalized engagement and transparent communication. Customers today want you to adapt to their buying journey and not for them to adapt to your sales process. This paradigm shift requires the salesperson to shed the old traditional tactics of selling and to embrace what I call **'unselling' and helping the customer buy.**

The Paradigm Shift:

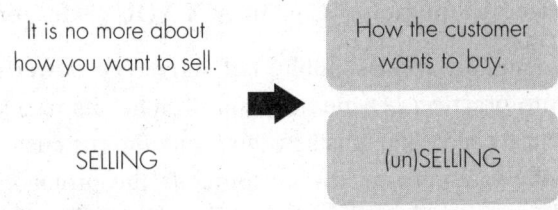

Unselling is the mantra for sales professionals to embrace the transformation in how we approach sales today. It's not about coercion or manipulation of your customer; it's about empowerment and collaboration. It is about acknowledging the changing dynamics of consumer behaviour, the rise of digital natives, embracing technology and the globalization of customers. It's about transcending the transactional mindset and fostering genuine connections with customers. It's the art of influence without imposition, the art of persuasion without pressure, and the art of selling by unselling.

I welcome you to the world of modern salesmanship, where your success will be determined **not by your ability to 'sell',** but by **your prowess in 'unselling'—in helping the customer buy.**

I have used this paradigm shift of unselling with a lot of

salespeople that I have trained across various industries and sectors globally to great success. The best part of unselling is that it becomes second nature once you understand and imbibe the underlying principle behind it, which is to *help* the customer buy.

In unselling, success is not just a destination, it's an ecosystem of collaboration, trust and understanding, and at the heart of this ecosystem lies a simple yet profound equation, which I like to call the **Success Equation** of the top salespeople.

Success Equation = Customer X YOU (Salesperson)

This equation seems simple, but it is very powerful when put into practice. Let me help you decipher its true strength! There are two protagonists in this equation: the customer and you, the salesperson. The customer is the protagonist with the dreams, needs and aspirations, and you, the salesperson, are the one who understands the customer's needs and has the skills to help them achieve their needs and aspirations. When you multiply them, it's like mixing the ingredients of a recipe and when combined properly, it results in something amazing, and in this case, it's success—for both the customer and the salesperson.

There is a caveat to this equation. A customer is someone you cannot control. You can influence him with your advice and guidance, but don't forget the customer has a mind of his own and will more often than not come with his own set of predefined notions into the sales equation. This is where 'your' skills as a trusted advisor and guide will play a crucial role in helping the customer make an informed decision on buying. However, the YOU part of the equation is completely in your control, and this is the part that, if you truly understand and master it, will increase your probability of success.

Research shows that 84% of business buyers expect sales reps to act as trusted advisors,[1] offering valuable guidance throughout the buying process. However, 59% of buyers feel that most sales reps don't take the time to truly understand their needs.[2] This disconnect plays a critical role in why deals fail, as it demonstrates that the salesperson's ability to engage and support the customer is a deciding factor in whether the sale is successful.

These statistics are crucial because they reveal a common misconception. Nearly 65% of sellers believe they always put the buyer first, but only 23% of buyers agree.[3] This significant gap highlights why rookie salespeople often jump to blame the customer when deals fall through. In reality, successful salespeople know that most of their success—just like the 84% of business buyers' expectations—depends on their ability to act as a trusted advisor and truly understand the customer's needs.[4]

This is a key takeaway that I want you to remember: nearly all of your success lies in your ability to effectively guide customers through their buying journey. The more you focus on being the advisor they expect, the more deals you'll close.

---

[1] 'State of the Connected Customer Report', *Salesforce*, https://tinyurl.com/5du9nydm. Accessed on 30 September 2024.
[2] Ibid.
[3] 'The State of Sales Report 2021', *LinkedIn Sales Solution*, 2021, https://tinyurl.com/5329fsnd. Accessed on 30 September 2024.
[4] Ibid.

What can you expect from this book, and who is it for?

I began selling at the age of 19, cold-calling customers and prospecting them into buying my product. Needless to say, apart from my passion, I had nothing to be successful in sales. No training, no tools, no guides or mentors to help navigate my first stint. Over the last twenty-plus years, I've had the fortune to work with, work under and collaborate with some of the best minds in sales around the world and across industries. I have studied them, learned from them, understanding the subtle nuances of what made them so successful in their careers. The sum of their and my years of experience is what I've tried to capture in this book.

Start Unselling Now is not just another sales manual; it's a manifesto for the modern sales professional, it's a manifesto for change. It is more than just a book—it's a journey of self-discovery and transformation, a companion on your quest for sales excellence.

Whether you're a novice seeking to lay a solid foundation or a seasoned veteran looking to reorient your approach, this book is for you. For beginners, it lays the foundation for mastering the art of unselling, providing practical insights and actionable strategies to kickstart their journey. For experienced salespeople, it offers a fresh perspective and a roadmap for reorienting their approach in alignment with the demands of the modern buyer. Everything in this will be covered from the point of view of our two protagonists, as mentioned above.

I've tried my best to cover and structure the key topics into simple frameworks and explain them with real-world examples. The end of every chapter is accompanied by a threefold learning and application methodology of **Reflect,**

Practise and Plan to help you put what you learn in theory in a practical context for you and your customers. It is meant to personalize the learning from others to how you can make it work for you and improve.

However, for the book to add real value to your sales career, I will need your help. As we embark on this journey on unselling, I want you to delve into the frameworks and methodologies presented in this book. But beyond mere theory, I want you to strive for a deeper understanding—an intuitive grasp of the principles at play. I want you to picture yourself in the scenarios described, reliving the challenges and celebrating the victories. Let the learning imparted here resonate with your experiences, guiding you towards those 'oh yea, it happened to me too' moments and occasional 'aha' revelations. I want you to turn this book into 'your book' of sales excellence and success.

So, are you ready to be challenged, inspired and transformed? Are you ready to embrace the power of unselling and revolutionize your approach to sales? If so, then join me on this exhilarating journey. The future of sales is here, and it begins with you.

Let's Start Unselling Now!

1

You, Your and Yourself

Why do you want to be in sales? That is a question I ask everyone I meet who is interested in becoming a salesperson. And every time the answer is 'for the money and the independence to make my own schedule'. Ask yourself why you want to be a salesperson. If your answer is the same as that of the thousands who have answered with the above, then you are right as well.

Almost everyone I know who has joined sales or is eager to join sales has heard of someone or knows someone who is extremely successful and wealthy doing sales. It's like watching Rafael Nadal or Kobe Bryant killing it on the court and you visualize yourself doing the same.

But what most people fail to visualize are the challenges, the hard work and the determination they will have to put in on a day-to-day basis towards honing their craft. How many times have those top salespersons failed yet found the courage to get up and keep moving forward until they made it to the top and even then, still continued to learn and get better?

Let us have a look at some interesting statistics about the sales industry, in general, so you know exactly what you are getting into and what it will take to succeed and be that top salesperson.

- 44% of salespeople give up after one follow-up call.[1]
- On average, it takes eight follow-up calls to reach a prospect.[2]
- 92% of salespeople give up after four 'no's', but 80% of prospects say 'no' four times before they say 'yes'.[3]
- 80% of sales require five follow-up calls.[4]
- Only 46.7% of sales reps globally meet their quota.[5]

No wonder a lot of newbies in sales give up in the first six months and the ones who stay focused and disciplined and persevere are the ones that make it to the top.

This brings me to the next big question for the 'you' part of the sales equation.

Who is a Salesperson?

How would you define a salesperson? There are a lot of classical definitions, such as: a salesperson is an individual who is responsible for selling products, services or solutions

---

[1] Ross, Lisa, 'The Importance of Sale Follow-Ups–Statistics', *Invesp*, 8 June 2019, https://tinyurl.com/482k2vfr. Accessed on 27 September 2024.

[2] Burdett, Eliot, '31 Must-Know Sales Follow-Up Statistics for 2024 Success', *Peak Sales Recruiting*, 21 December 2023, https://tinyurl.com/3dunscpw. Accessed on 27 September 2024.

[3] Clay, Robert, 'Why You Must Follow up Leads', *Marketing Donut*, https://tinyurl.com/3b2vx4ws. Accessed on 27 September 2024.

[4] Assemi, Ramin, '55 Shocking Sales Statistics That'll Change the Way You Sell in 2024', *Close*, 8 December 2023, https://tinyurl.com/439dc27h. Accessed on 27 September 2024.

[5] Connaughton, Brendan, '135 Essential Sales Statistics You Need to Know in 2024', *Qwilr*, 26 February 2024, https://tinyurl.com/5e7mkvyj. Accessed on 27 September 2024.

to customers on behalf of a company or organization.

OR

A salesperson is someone who engages with potential customers, understands their needs and preferences, and effectively communicates the value and benefits of the products or services they are selling.

These definitions are not wrong, but in my many years of experience, I have realized that we look at these definitions from the wrong point of view. Let me explain with an analogy and a lesson I got from an expert when I was nineteen years old.

If I tell you a Formula One race car driver is a very fast car driver, your instant reaction to that would be, 'Obviously! For someone who wins sometimes by a margin of less than 1/10th of a second, he has to be damn fast. But that is not how you would define a Formula One car driver because driving fast and having fast reflexes is a given for that role.' And you would be right in saying that.

When I was 19 years old, I had the opportunity to visit the Sepang Grand Prix Circuit in Malaysia and meet the engineers of some of the racing teams. What fascinated me was understanding what differentiates the best from the best when driving fast and quick reflexes are pretty much a given, since they are competing in the world's fastest racing car competition.

One of the engineers there said something which I remember to this day. He said, 'You need to understand who the driver is. By that, I don't mean just who is driving the car, but rather it is a combination of that person's attributes, skills and mindset that makes him a world-class driver, and we work around him to make sure he gets to the podium.' The whole strategy is built around maximizing that. He explained further, saying that at that time, there were only three drivers in Formula One who would burn out on average an extra pair of tyres because their driving style was aggressive on corners, breaking last to get a chance to pull up that extra one-tenth of a second from other drivers.

What this meant for the team was that they had to have an extra pit stop for these drivers, which, if you follow Formula One, you will know is a decision between finishing in the lead or in the middle of the pack. But that clear and deep understanding of the driver's psyche and his mindset was what led the driver and team to be so successful.

So, coming to our definition as to who is a salesperson, I always look at this from the 'person' perspective first. And I want you also to look at it that way. Do not fall into the trap of emulating the classical definition of a successful salesperson without deep diving into knowing the person, which is you in this case.

In all of my years of coaching salespeople, I have always said that sales skills can be acquired, and I can help you learn that, but I cannot change who you are as a person. Who you are as a person is the foundation over which all skill sets can be built. But it starts with YOU first—the person in Salesperson.

I like to break down and define a salesperson as the person first, followed closely by his personality (which, in this case, also denotes the skills that they need to buy), and finally, the sales part.

As we go through the chapter, I will break down the term salesperson into three elements—**Person, Personality and Sales**—to help you understand these in detail and enable you to grasp what it takes to be a great salesperson a little better.

PERSON: The First Element

Every person has some fundamental qualities, which, as I said before, lay the foundation for who the person is. Though I have massive respect for wolves, from my experience I have always found bear to be more suited to describe the person when it comes to sales.

BEAR: Believer, Ethical, Ambitious and Resilient

You cannot make a customer buy anything if you don't believe in the product or service you are pitching. The belief and conviction of a sale is the first step to closing a sale. This also brings me to an important point. Never try to sell any service or product that you don't believe in. Remember, if you are not convinced about it, you will not be able to convince the customer, and the customer will see right through that.

Many years ago, I had a team member who was selling luxury properties. Despite being very disciplined and diligent, he was struggling to make any sales. Countless follow-ups and visits to the site and the result was still the same. One day, we spoke about the challenges he was facing to try and find a solution.

I asked him, 'Imagine if you were a very wealthy guy and had all the money in the world, which property in the luxury project would you buy?'

He replied, 'I won't buy this property, as with this amount of money, I can buy four houses, which is more value for my money.'

Now, the answer he gave was not wrong, but it highlighted the problem he was having. He **didn't believe** in the product himself. He could not believe why someone would want to spend so much money on a luxury house, and his own doubts were hindering him from pitching to the customers. Luxury sales, a lot of times, are not about pitching the benefits or the USP of a product or service. Luxury sales are about how that product will fit into the existing lifestyle of the customer.

I suggested he move to the mid-segment property and rental division. The move did wonders for him, and in just six months, he went from being a sales agent to becoming a sales manager and leading a team under him.

Belief in what you are selling is a great catalyst in lighting up your pitch and energy when you are speaking to the customer. As at that, it is very easy for you to put yourself in their shoes and feel comfortable.

The next quality from 'Bear', which is very personal and critical to me, is ethics. I have always kept a zero-tolerance policy towards unethical salespeople. It is better to have an average hardworking salesperson who is ethical than a rockstar salesperson who lacks ethics. Ethics define the character of the person who would work alongside you, and a lot of times, sales becomes a tag team challenge. Like any successful team, you would want the person in your team to be ethical and trustworthy.

Why I give a lot of importance to ethics also comes from the fact that over my years in sales, I have encountered a lot of fallacies, myths and fake bravado statements that get misconstrued as great salesmanship.

Some examples like, 'He is such a strong sales guy that he can sell a comb to a bald guy!' There are many variations of this statement across the world, and I am sure you must have heard them.

Let me just say that such a salesperson is NOT a strong salesperson. Selling is not about conning the customer. You might make one or two deals, but very soon, you will become one of those statistics of salespeople who quit because no one wants to deal with them.

Sales as a career is not a short game. If you ask any successful salesperson, they will tell you it is a lot of hard work, a lot of dedication, and the immense trust put in them by their customers that made them so successful. NOT EVEN ONE will say it's because they were great con artists scamming customers.

Ethics is one of the major foundations you need to build your sales career on if you want to be successful and reach the top.

The next quality I want to talk about is ambition. Great Roman Emperor Marcus Aurelius once said, 'A man's worth is no greater than his ambitions.'

Ambition to achieve big, ambition to dream big, and ambition to be very successful in sales is the first step in getting the right attitude and paving the first brick in your journey to sales success.

Of course, this big ambition needs to be backed with an equal, if not bigger, action to make it a reality. Keep your ambitions so high that the average seems too low a benchmark, as aiming for the average is a 100% proven recipe for failure.

If your ambitions sound ridiculous to others, take it from me that you are on the right path. Back it up with relentless action, and everyone will take notice.

Let me give you two examples that I distinctly remember of how ambition sets you on the path to success. Many years ago, when I worked in an FMCG or consumer goods company, at our half-yearly national sales meeting, we were conducting a business performance review. As part of the review, the targets for the balance of the year were also discussed. One after the other, the state heads had their targets anywhere from a growth of 15–20%, which is considered quite good for a big-scale consumer goods company. A young state head in the meeting mentioned he wanted to take a target of two times growth in the next six months in his state. His statement was met with silence, followed by ridicule from some of the senior veterans of other states, citing that the young gun was trying to bite more than he could chew.

Once the meeting was over, I spoke to our commercial director and wanted to get his take on this target set by the young state head. His answer was simple. He said it takes guts to sit amidst veterans of sales and take a target so massive and be the subject of ridicule yet keep one's composure. He said, and I remember like it was yesterday, 'Even if he achieves half of what he targeted, he is still a winner as he took on the ambition to think beyond the normal growth that other veterans have taken. He will end up finding ways never explored before, and that will lead him to leap way beyond others in subsequent quarters.'

Lo and behold, the end of the quarter came, and the results were in. The young state head hit 2.2 times growth and all of his sales managers ended up being in the top five sales managers nationwide. That ambition set the tone for success not just for him and his managers under him but also for the entire company as it forced everyone to think beyond the standard norms of 15–20% growth. So, his ambition followed by rigorous action did end up opening up ways that were never explored before.

Here is another example of how ambition or lack of

ambition can set the mindset and your trajectory in sales. If you've been in sales, I am sure you have come across such people as well. I have seen salespeople who plan their sales based on commission and how long it will last them comfortably, and then they draw the line for action there. These are the people who say, 'If I close one deal, the commission will help me last for two weeks easily, so I focus on closing two deals a month, and my life is sorted.' This is a classic example of a lack of ambition limiting their mindset and their desire for action, and this is the formula that leads to being just average.

In contrast, successful salespeople want to close as many deals as possible and want to keep repeating them day after day, week after week, month after month and year after year. Their ambition to be at the top builds their mindset to drive more and more action, ensuring they are not content with average sales or just above average. They set their own benchmark, which is usually way above the average line.

An easy way to remember this is to keep in mind the image below.

Big ambitions, despite being followed by big actions, will still lead to a lot of failures, rejections and disappointments. There is not a single successful person in any field or industry, let alone sales, who has not failed. So, it WILL happen to you too. You will also fail, you will also get rejected, and you will also be disappointed, I can guarantee that. But what will set you apart from the others is your resilience to keep finding and exploring ways until you achieve your ambitions.

> *One of the best predictors of ultimate success...isn't natural talent or even industry expertise, but how do you explain your failures and rejections.*
>
> —DANIEL H. PINK

If ambition is one side of the coin, then resilience is easily the other side to balance it. We have all heard of the famous story of how Michael Jordan was not even selected for his school team, but his resilience, matched with his ambitions and actions, eventually made him the G.O.A.T. of the sport.

Oftentimes, people say that to be successful in sales, you have to be 'thick-skinned'. If you look up in a dictionary what this phrase means, it says 'not easily bothered by criticism or insult'.

This does not mean that successful salespeople have learned to ignore the criticism; rather, they understand that a customer's choice to not buy from you is not a reflection of you as a person, but instead, this is a way for customers to give feedback on points where you still need to improve and do a better job. So, they pick themselves up from there, learn about the gaps, fill them, and go back to it again.

One of the quotes from the movie *Rocky Balboa* summarizes this very nicely:

It ain't about how hard ya hit. It's about how hard you can get hit and keep moving forward. How much you can take and keep moving forward. That's how winning is done!

—SYLVESTER STALLONE, *Rocky Balboa*

PERSONALITY—The Second Element

Now that we understand the 'person' in salesperson, let's have a look at the individual's personality, which enables him to succeed in this profession. I like to call the personality traits **CLASP** as an easy way to remember.

CLASP here stands for:

a) <u>C</u>ustomer first and customer until the end
b) <u>L</u>earning continuously
c) <u>A</u>dapting to change
d) <u>S</u>toryteller (and a great one at that)
e) <u>P</u>ersistent, but NOT pushy

In sales, everything **starts and ends with the customer.** It *starts* with understanding the needs of the customer and *ends* when the customer finally buys your product by paying for it. So, the customer is the anchor point around which everything is centred or built. They are the driving force behind every interaction, every transaction, and every success. Hence, it is paramount to keep the 'customer always first' in mind.

It sounds as obvious as much as it is ignored by salespeople. Oftentimes, salespeople think it's a game of probability, and the goal is to try and reach out to as many customers as possible, and some will convert anyway. I can tell you from experience that this is a fallacy. While you will never be able to close all deals with customers, that does not mean you should not treat each customer uniquely and with focus.

Remember to deal with each customer as if he is your only customer. That is the only way to really keep the 'customer first' in your approach.

Some common mistakes salespeople make during their handling of customers or potential leads is when they start with the customer-first approach, and as the sales process goes on, they lose focus on keeping the customer approach until the deal is closed. Many times, it gets into the mode of making excuses about the customer not responding or the lead is not hot, or anything but the salesperson's fault, thereby eventually losing focus on 'keeping the customer first and until the end' approach. This is also the reason for many times deals not getting closed.

Let me explain what it actually means from an execution perspective, what it means to be 'customer first and until the end' focused. From the moment you engage with a potential customer to the final stage of closing a deal, your focus should be centred on understanding and fulfilling their needs and expectations.

At the beginning of any sales process, it is crucial to understand deeply the customer's pain points, desires and goals. This helps you to develop a comprehensive understanding of their unique challenges, enabling you to present a solution that directly addresses their specific needs. By putting the customer at the forefront of the sales process, you lay the foundation for a successful and mutually beneficial partnership.

As the sales process progresses, it is essential to

continuously prioritize the customer's satisfaction. This involves maintaining open lines of communication, providing prompt responses and proactively addressing any concerns or issues that may arise. By consistently demonstrating that their needs and preferences matter, you can build trust and foster a positive customer experience. Additionally, if you go the extra mile to exceed their expectations, whether it's by providing additional resources, offering personalized recommendations or delivering exceptional post-sale support, you ensure that the customer feels valued and supported throughout their journey. This leads to the cultivation of long-term relationships and customer loyalty.

Remember, 'the buyer buys into you before buying your product or service'. And if the customer feels supported, helped and advised correctly throughout their journey, they have no reason not to 'buy' into you, which is quickly followed by buying your product or service.

This customer-centric approach not only fosters stronger relationships but also leads to positive word-of-mouth referrals, which will further enhance your reputation as a sales professional.

We will uncover more examples and methods in the later chapters in detail to practise this deeper, but for now, remember to always keep the customer first until the end when your deal is closed. With this, you will lay the foundation for a strong and successful sales career.

Anyone who stops learning is old, whether at twenty or eighty. Anyone who keeps learning stays young.

—HENRY FORD

Top salespeople are always learning.

In the world of sales, adopting an **always-learning mindset** is crucial for growth and success. Personally, I believe that every interaction, whether it results in a sale or not, presents an opportunity to learn and improve. By approaching each situation as an opportunity for knowledge, you can continuously enhance your skills, adapt to new trends, and better serve your customers.

If you think of it pragmatically, every salesperson pitching to a customer is pitching with the mindset that they are the subject matter expert in that domain and hence the best suited to advise, guide or help the customer in making the right choice. To maintain that expertise in a dynamic field such as sales, you need to be in an always-learning mindset.

Sales is a dynamic field, and staying ahead of the curve is essential to provide value to your customers. Whether it is reading industry publications, attending relevant webinars or conferences, or engaging in networking opportunities, you should stay informed about the latest innovations, challenges and best practices. This will enable you to bring fresh insights to your customers and position you as a trusted advisor to the customer and a genuine subject matter expert they look forward to interacting with.

Another aspect of continuous learning in sales is seeking feedback and actively reflecting on your performance. After each interaction or sales pitch, take the time to review what went well and identify areas for improvement. This self-assessment helps you refine your approach, identify patterns and adapt your strategies based on the feedback received. Additionally, actively seek feedback from colleagues, mentors and even customers themselves. Constructive criticism is a valuable tool for growth, and by embracing it with an open mind, you can refine your skills and deliver even better results.

I always speak about customer feedback as the best learning tool for any salesperson.

> The best customer feedback is when the customer does not buy from you.

We will cover this in more detail and understand how to listen to this feedback and learn from it in the subsequent chapters.

In the ever-changing world of sales, **developing an adaptable mindset** is crucial for your success. One recent and significant example of adapting to change is the impact of the COVID-19 pandemic on the sales ecosystem. The pandemic disrupted traditional sales practices, such as in-person meetings and trade shows. This took away the opportunity to meet your customers in person and see their reactions face to face. As a result, people had to pivot their approach and embrace virtual selling methods—from quickly adapting by leveraging video conferencing platforms to conducting sales meetings and presentations remotely. By embracing this change and mastering virtual selling techniques, top salespeople were still able to engage with clients, foster relationships, and close deals despite the challenging circumstances.

Another aspect of adapting to change in sales is the evolving buyer behaviour. We are living in times where you have everyone from the Baby Boomers, Gen X and Millennials to Gen Z as your customers. Their buying behaviour and needs vary across a vast spectrum, and hence, your pitch and your approach will also need to be adapted accordingly as you deal with them.

Furthermore, today's buyers are more informed as they conduct extensive research online, read reviews and compare prices before making any purchasing decisions. To adapt and become successful in this changing landscape, you must step up and become a trusted advisor to the customer rather than a traditional salesperson. Let's not forget that technological advancements, such as artificial intelligence and automation, have transformed various aspects of sales processes. Social media platforms like LinkedIn, X (earlier known as Twitter) and Facebook offer a multitude of opportunities for sales professionals to connect with prospects and build relationships. To leverage this changing trend, you will have to adapt and become proficient and embrace these platforms and mediums as powerful tools for prospecting and networking so you can expand your reach, engage with a wider audience, and ultimately generate more leads and sales.

 We will cover the practical adaptation to technology and how to leverage it effectively in a later chapter.

We are all storytellers. We all live in a network of stories. There isn't a stronger connection between people than storytelling.

—JIMMY NEIL SMITH

The action of making a purchase may seem like a transaction, but the action point that leads to that moment is always triggered by emotions—the emotional connection of the customer's needs to the product or service, the salesperson, or the value they believe they will derive out of using that product or service. And there is no better way of connecting with people and evoking those emotions than through the art of effective storytelling. I firmly believe top salespeople are great storytellers. They have mastered the art of making the customer visualize and connect with the salesperson's storytelling (pitch).

Mastering the **art of effective storytelling** is a powerful tool that can elevate your success. By incorporating storytelling into your sales approach, you can engage your prospects and customers on a deeper level, evoke emotions, and ultimately influence their buying decisions. For example, imagine you are selling a luxury travel package. Instead of simply listing the features and amenities, you weave a story of a couple celebrating their anniversary on an idyllic island getaway. By painting a picture of their unforgettable experiences, the romantic sunsets and the personalized service, you transport your prospects into the narrative, allowing them to envision themselves enjoying a similar experience. Effective storytelling makes the customer visualize themselves as the protagonist of that story.

Moreover, effective storytelling can be a valuable tool for building credibility and trust. By sharing authentic stories of satisfied customers who have experienced success with your product or service, you create social proof and instil confidence in your prospects. For instance, you may narrate the story of a business owner who increased their revenue by implementing your software solution. By showcasing tangible results and the positive impact on real people, you strengthen your credibility and demonstrate the value of your offering.

Another aspect of effective storytelling in sales is aligning your narratives with the pain points and aspirations of your audience. By understanding their challenges and aspirations, you can craft stories that resonate with their specific needs. For instance, if you are selling a productivity tool to busy professionals, you may share a story of a time-strapped executive who transformed their work-life balance and achieved greater productivity by utilizing your solution. By addressing their specific pain points and presenting a relatable success story, you establish a connection and position yourself as a problem solver.

Furthermore, effective storytelling is not limited to product or service narratives alone. It can also be employed to convey your brand's values, vision and mission. By sharing stories that embody your brand's ethos, you create an emotional connection with your audience. For example, you might narrate the story of how your company started with a humble vision and grew to become a leader in the industry, all the while maintaining a commitment to its customers' needs as the anchor and always listening to the customer's feedback to evolve and adapt. By aligning your brand's story with your audience's values, you forge a deeper connection and differentiate yourself from competitors.

In the context of virtual selling during the COVID-19 pandemic, effective storytelling has become even more important. With limited face-to-face interaction, virtual platforms provide an opportunity to engage your audience on a personal level. Imagine that while delivering a sales presentation over video conferencing, you leverage storytelling techniques to make your message memorable and impactful. By sharing real-life customer success stories or narrating relatable scenarios, you can connect with your prospects and build trust, even in the absence of physical presence. Storytelling allows you to bridge the gap and create a human connection in virtual space.

> *Nothing in this world can take the place of persistence. Nothing is more common than unsuccessful men with talent. Persistence and determination alone are omnipotent.*
>
> —CALVIN COOLIDGE

> *Ambition is the path to success.*
> *Persistence is the vehicle you arrive in.*
>
> —BILL BRADLEY

Persistence is defined as 'firm or obstinate continuance in a **course of action** in spite of difficulty or opposition'. It is crucial in building long-term relationships with your clients. However, many times, it gets confused with being pushy by new salespeople. Whenever I try to talk about persistence as a trait of a successful salesperson, I always highlight 'pushy' and explain the difference between them.

How many times have you personally dreaded meeting salespeople or taking their calls and commenting that they are just very pushy? The difference lies in how a salesperson interprets and handles the 'course of action' mentioned above in the definition. And the difference is simple. A **persistent** salesperson is interested in helping the buyer with any doubts they still have, helping them make that decision. In contrast, a **pushy** salesperson is only interested in getting his sales done as quickly as possible, thereby looking aggressive and putting his benefits over the customer's needs.

Persistence, when done right, involves consistent follow-ups and staying engaged with your prospects. For example, you may schedule regular check-ins, provide valuable resources or insights, and offer assistance whenever needed. The key is to maintain a respectful and helpful attitude, ensuring that your persistence is driven by a genuine desire to assist and provide value to your prospects.

On the other hand, being pushy involves applying undue pressure, disregarding the needs or preferences of your prospects, and pursuing a sale at any cost. This approach can damage trust and harm the relationship. It's important to recognize and respect the boundaries set by your prospects. If a prospect has clearly indicated disinterest or asked for space, being pushy is counterproductive and can lead to negative outcomes.

A key aspect of differentiating persistence from being pushy is actively listening to your prospects. By attentively understanding their needs, concerns and timelines, you can tailor your approach and adapt your persistence accordingly. This demonstrates empathy and respect for their decision-making process. If a prospect expresses that they require more time or have specific concerns, adapt your strategy and offer support without being forceful or imposing.

In most sales transactions, it is rare to close a deal after just one interaction. Oftentimes, it takes multiple touchpoints and follow-ups to move a prospect through the sales funnel. By consistently staying in touch and nurturing relationships, you can build trust and credibility over time. A smart way of doing this is by scheduling regular check-ins, providing updates on industry trends, or sharing valuable resources that align with your clients' needs. By staying persistent in your efforts to build and maintain relationships, you position yourself as a reliable and trusted partner who is more interested in helping the customer buy, rather than selling to the customer. So always be mindful and **be persistent rather than pushy** with your customers and prospects.

SALES—The Final Element

For the final element of the 'sales' part in the definition, I would like to start with a common mistake made by most rookie salespeople. This is also a misconception that many people who choose sales as a career have. The swanky lines in a movie or the bashful way of converting the customers into numbers or deals is NOT what sales is about. Rather, sales is about humanizing your customer. If you don't humanize your customers, you won't be able to understand, connect or empathize with their needs, which simply will hinder you in helping your customers buy. Treating your customer as a number will trap you in a never-ending loop of probability and statistics, preventing you from becoming a true salesperson, let alone a great salesperson.

Keeping this humanizing style of dealing with customers is why I like to use the 'CARES' approach. It has always helped me focus and reminded me of what it actually means when I think about sales and my prospective customers, and the means to make the customer buy rather than to sell to him.

The CARES Approach

The CARES approach will help you keep the customer always in the core focus and the best part about this approach is that it is very logical and obvious as this is exactly how you would want to be dealt with as a customer yourself.

CARES stands for Customer-centric approach, Active listening, Resourceful problem-solver, Exemplary customer service and Seamless customer journey.

a) Customer-Centric Approach

CARES

Ask any successful salesperson, and they will tell you that putting the customer at the centre of every interaction is paramount. By adopting a customer-centric approach, you prioritize understanding and fulfilling the needs and wants of your customers. This involves probing the needs of the customer and their concerns and pain points. Once you have figured out the real needs and aspirations of your customer, you can tailor your solutions to address their specific requirements. This not only makes the customer's buying process simplified but also demonstrates that you genuinely care about their success and satisfaction, positioning you as a trusted advisor.

b) Active Listening

CARES

Active listening is a crucial ability that enables you to fully comprehend your consumers and their particular difficulties. It entails listening to what they say and also observing their tone, body language and underlying wants. You can confirm your comprehension of the client's needs and demonstrate your appreciation for their feedback by actively listening to them. This increases the likelihood of a successful sale by enabling you to establish a stronger rapport with them and match your offerings with their unique pain areas. In order to offer a full solution, active listening also enables you to identify supplementary wants or concealed worries that the consumer may not have directly mentioned.

c) Resourceful Problem-Solver

CARES

As a sales professional, having a resourceful mindset is crucial for coming up with creative answers to your clients' problems. You can find novel approaches to deal with their problems by exercising your imagination and making use of your knowledge and experience. This necessitates maintaining current market trends, being completely familiar with your product or service, and using creative thinking. Solving problems creatively requires more than just promoting a good product or service. It entails actively looking for possibilities to add value by coming up with complementary solutions or discovering fresh approaches to assist the client in achieving their objectives. You may develop enduring relationships with your clients and establish yourself as a go-to resource for them by being reliable and their issue solver.

d) Exemplary Customer Service

CARES

In the competitive sales environment, providing exceptional customer service sets you apart and makes you unique. Going above and beyond to provide a personalized experience shows that you care about keeping your customers happy. It entails being receptive, giving timely information that is accurate, and foreseeing their needs before they ever become apparent. Delivering outstanding customer service requires having effective communication skills. When you communicate clearly and succinctly, it's easier to explain the value of your services, respond to inquiries, and allay any fears that customers might have. In order to make sure the consumer feels supported throughout the sales process, it means proactive and prompt follow-up. You build loyal advocates who are more likely to refer your goods or services to others, by developing strong connections with your consumers based on trust, transparency and dependability.

e) Seamless Customer Journey

From the first point of contact to the last sale and beyond, the customer experience should be frictionless and seamless. It involves making sure that each interaction with your clients is effectively managed and enhances their experience. Streamlining communication, offering prompt and relevant follow-ups, and giving dependable support are all part of this. By making the customer journey as smooth as possible, you build trust, reduce customer churn, and increase the likelihood of repeat business.

We will dive deeper into the CARES approach as we go through the book, going into details and learning about each topic through examples to help you create your own personalized blueprint for sales success.

Now that we have explored the foundational qualities of a successful salesperson, let's move on to applying these insights. The following Reflect, Practise and Plan sections will help you internalize and act upon the BEAR and CLASP characteristics.

🐻 REFLECT

- How do your personal qualities (BEAR: Believer, Ethical, Ambitious, Resilient) influence your sales approach? Rate yourself honestly from one to five, and anything below a rating of four is something that needs to be worked on.

- Consider how the CLASP characteristics impact your interactions with customers. Can you identify and note down a recent sales interaction where these traits were evident?
- Assess and write down which CLASP characteristic you find most challenging and why.

PRACTISE

- Practise applying the CARES approach in a simulated sales scenario. Focus on one element at a time to see its direct impact on the interaction.
- Role-play a sales scenario where you emphasize each of the CLASP traits. Record and review the outcomes to identify areas for improvement.

PLAN

- In your next five customer interactions, focus on one CLASP element and record the results. How did focusing on this element change the interaction?
- Select one of the BEAR qualities (where you rated yourself less than four) and practise it in your interactions this week. Note any changes in customer responses or sales outcomes.
- Develop a weekly checklist to assess how well you are incorporating the CARES approach into your daily sales activities.

2

Your Customer

Now we come to the second critical part of the aforementioned sales equation, the customer. Everyone has heard the famous sayings, 'Customer is king' or 'The customer is always right'. This doesn't lead to the 'king' being treated as such. In fact, more often than not, salespeople fail to understand the customer properly.

Before we get into the details in the chapter, I want to explain how understanding the customer can lead to your success as a salesperson.

In the previous chapter, we discussed everything about you as a salesperson, your personality traits and the skills needed to succeed as a sales professional. But all of that is useless if we are unable to apply it in the right context and in an optimum way.

The importance of this chapter on the customer is paramount as it will enable you to understand and then adapt to your customer and help him buy more successfully. It's like how a doctor needs to understand all aspects of a visiting patient before he gives his diagnosis.

A doctor needs to take into consideration everything, from environmental factors prevailing in the city to your diet, medical history, body composition, current symptoms, allergies, insurance status, etc., before coming up with a treatment plan. Imagine if the doctor would give everyone the same seven or eight generic drugs, regardless of the symptoms, what would your perspective or feedback be regarding the doctor? That he is inexperienced, a fraud, or not a real doctor.

Similarly, as a sales professional (though it is not a life-or-death situation), it is very important to understand your customer from all aspects—their fears or concerns, needs and wants, motivations, preference of communication, decision trigger, etc.—before you adapt your approach to help or advise the customer in the right way.

As simple and obvious as it sounds, a majority of salespeople make a mistake here, and when the customer stops responding to their follow-ups, the excuse becomes blaming the customer. Where in reality the root cause of this nine out of ten times would be the gap in our approach to handling the customer. Sales professionals, under the pressure of closing sales, start applying the same memorized pitch with the same benefits, in the same tone and pace, to every customer they meet or speak to, whether in person or virtually. Remember that different customers can purchase the same product for entirely different reasons, hence your pitch or approach has to be adapted accordingly.

Recent research suggests that a customer moves through more than five touchpoints before making a purchase. Today's customer is well informed, well researched, and uses multiple touchpoints or channels to know more about the product or the service they are seeking. Add to this the complexity of handling customers across different generations, from Baby Boomers to Generation Z, also known as Gen Z. In some industries, we are even talking about Gen Alpha. This has led to a major shift in the customer paradigm.

It is no longer about keeping the right product at the right place and right time but also across the right touchpoints, ensuring a seamless customer journey through the customer's preferred mode of communication. In short, **it is no more about how you want to sell to the customer, but rather how the customer wants to buy today.**

This paradigm shift is the reality in sales today, and the big question is how you adapt to it to become successful. The answer to that lies in changing our approach to our customers. You have to move beyond the old paradigm of just '**Knowing your Customer (KYC)**' to '**Understand your Customer (UYC)**' and then to '**Adapt to your Customer (AYC)**'.

The **New Paradigm** of understanding customers:

$$KYC \longrightarrow UYC \longrightarrow AYC$$

To understand this transition better, I will take you through it in a logical flow to ensure that you are ready to handle any kind of customer and use that to tailor-make your approach to helping them buy.

The new paradigm is a logical flow of understanding your customer, and I have coached many sales professionals with this, yielding great results. As we go through this in detail, you will see how in today's modern world, salespeople encounter various types of customers, each with their unique characteristics and preferences. Understanding the different customer types can help salespeople tailor their approach, from pitching to adapting their communication strategies, leading to building effective relationships.

Dissecting the paradigm into four main parts:

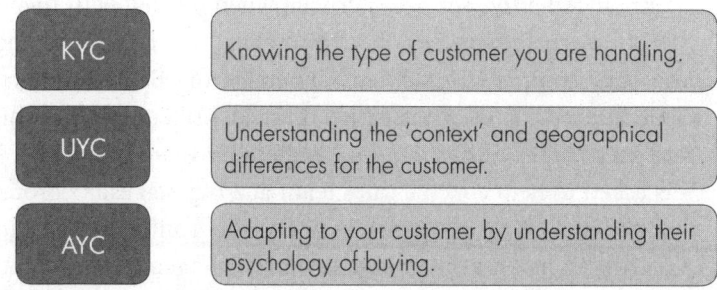

- **KYC**: Knowing the type of customer you are handling.
- **UYC**: Understanding the 'context' and geographical differences for the customer.
- **AYC**: Adapting to your customer by understanding their psychology of buying.

KYC   Knowing the Types of Customers

Knowing your customer, or KYC in today's terminology, has become such an overused term that a lot of times, people miss the essence of what KYC actually is. It is not about just knowing the personal details of the customer but rather about understanding what type of customer you are handling. It goes way beyond knowing the customer's name, age, income and such details. I mentioned before about today's customers spanning from Baby Boomers to Gen Z. Knowing the type of customer will help you understand them better.

Below are some common types of customers you may encounter.

The Traditional Customer

These customers typically prefer a more **traditional approach** to buying. They value **face-to-face interactions and personal relationships, relying on word-of-mouth recommendations** or social proof when making their decisions. Hence, it becomes more critical to establish trust and rapport through personalized attention. Attentive service is crucial when dealing with them.

These customers will buy into you first before buying into your company or service. Generally, the Baby Boomers, Generation X or even an earlier part of Millennials will fall into these types of customers. I remember many years ago, I was asked to help coach a sales team at a big real estate group that had just set up an agency in one of the frontier markets in Asia, which had a very unorganized rental agency ecosystem. One of the first things I prioritized in the team as part of the sales training was the mandate of in-person etiquette while dealing with the customers. Some of the things in those were dressing up in suits when meeting the customers (now, it may seem very intuitive and obvious but remember this is a frontier market with no organized setup or regulations), reminding the customer prior to the meeting, and sending a brief 'thank you' note post the meeting and the details discussed.

I can tell you, like most salespeople, they too thought it to be ridiculous as they believed the ultimate objective was to sell or rent property, and that all these other things I mentioned were mere gimmicks and would take up too much of their time. We ran this for four weeks as a must for the entire team. The average number of viewings per agent per week increased from nine viewings to more than 22 per week, and the response rate from the customers during the follow-up calls almost tripled.

All this finally became clear to them when a Japanese customer gave a testimonial to one of the agents stating that he never imagined in a country (where the agency was) like that, the agents would be so professionally dressed and prompt, and he felt absolutely confident in the choices and advice he was given and shown by the agent. Needless to say, the agency started converting a lot more prospects than previously. Like I said, the customers bought into the agent first before they bought into the product or service.

> We will be using this identification in later chapters to tailor our approaches as we go into pitch, communication and other topics, so bookmark this page.

The Digital Native Customer

Digital natives are customers who are highly **tech-savvy and comfortable with online interactions**. They prefer digital channels for researching the products they need, evaluating options, making purchases and seeking customer support. Salespeople who are dealing with digital natives should be adept at utilizing technology, providing seamless online experiences, and leveraging social media and digital marketing strategies to engage with this customer segment.

These customers are generally from the Millennial generation to the current Generation Z. They are comfortable with the information overload of options and prefer doing their own research before reaching out to sales professionals. They have very targeted questions that they want the sales professionals to answer; they have already done quite a bit of research on their own and seek direct, short and crisp answers to their queries.

So, the salesperson has to be well informed, not just about their own product or service but also about other competitors in the market, so as to give a fair evaluation and differentiate the USPs of their own products. Repeating the information that is readily available online is not the way to add value for these customers. Rather, as a smart salesperson, you should focus on helping them differentiate with ease among the options with your expertise and, more importantly, add the other benefits that they will get which are not mentioned online.

Even your communication strategies might change as these types of customers are very comfortable with getting the information through virtual channels or short messaging platforms, so they can evaluate themselves and get back to you with more doubts. In a lot of cases, you will play a strong role of being their assistant in finding the choice among all options and occasionally nudging them with your 'clear and concise' points of differentiation for them to act on.

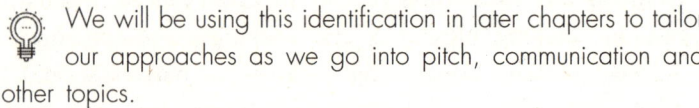 We will be using this identification in later chapters to tailor our approaches as we go into pitch, communication and other topics.

The Value-Seeking Customer

Value seekers, simply put, **are price-conscious customers who prioritize getting the best possible deal**. They meticulously compare prices, features and benefits before making a purchase decision. These types of customers will generally prioritize their functional needs for a service or product over the 'preferred wants' if they get a better value-for-money deal.

The key when handling such customers is to focus on demonstrating the value proposition, highlighting cost savings and offering competitive pricing or discounts to win over value seekers. An easy way to also identify them is when you're pitching, these customers will jump to asking and comparing prices once they understand the functional features among the options that more or less fit their needs. A good technique to be used by sales professionals is to smartly emphasize the value proposition of your product and service and, at the same time, probe for their 'additional wants' apart from the functional needs.

This information can be used as an additional nudge to tip the customer over towards your product vs. the competitors, as you would be providing not just the value proposition at the best possible price, but to add icing to the cake, you would also be satisfying some of their additional wants as a pleasant 'surprise'.

Remember that these customers are generally tough negotiators, but once you show them the 'value' they are seeking at the best price and couple that with the 'surprise' mentioned above, it will generally help you to win them over.

> We will be using this identification in later chapters to tailor our approaches as we go into pitch, communication and other topics.

The Relationship-Driven Customer

Relationship buyers **prioritize long-term partnerships and value the trust and connection they have with a salesperson or a brand**. They prefer personalized attention, proactive communication and exceptional customer service. These types of customers do not shop around multiple sources once they find a reliable and trustworthy advisor to guide them through the entire buying journey.

Salespeople handling such customers should invest time in building strong relationships, understanding the buyer's preferences, and going the extra mile to exceed expectations to maintain loyalty. These customers value the relationship and the personalized service they get from the sales professional and like to stick to the same salesperson for all their needs, leading to a lot of repeat business.

Customers like these are generally known to be good brand ambassadors for the product or service, and more importantly, they also enhance the credibility of the sales professional through word-of-mouth recommendations. Needless to say, these customers are the highest source of referrals, which not only makes the prospect pipeline for the salesperson full but also helps to convert faster.

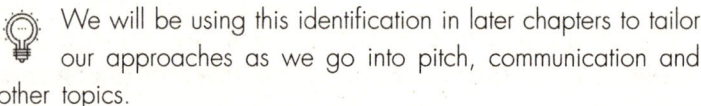 We will be using this identification in later chapters to tailor our approaches as we go into pitch, communication and other topics.

The Collaborative Customer

Collaborative buyers are the type of customers who **prefer a cooperative and consultative approach when it comes to making a purchase decision**. They actively participate in the sales process, engage in discussions, and value salespeople who act as trusted advisors. They value transparency, open communication and collaborative problem-solving. These types of customers are generally very understanding and will work alongside salespeople to find the optimum solution.

Salespeople handling this type of customer should engage in consultative selling, actively listen to their needs and preferences, and involve them in product demonstrations, trials or customization processes. Dealing with them and providing a personalized solution to meet their specific needs requires a bit of effort, but the positive part of this is that throughout the process, the customer is actively assisted and collaborates in reaching the solution.

Collaborative customers are very good for salespeople who are trying to enter a new market with a product and service and need someone to pilot it. As these customers are collaborative, they are also willing to experiment and work alongside in using the solution and assist the salesperson to get the right fit as needed.

I have coached some SaaS company sales leadership on working with such customers as part of their Go-to-Market (GTM) strategy, as it allows the team to set the product for the right fit in the market, all with the support of the collaborative customer and their feedback.

> We will be using this identification in later chapters to tailor our approaches as we go into pitch, communication and other topics.

It's important to note that these customer types are not mutually exclusive, and individuals may exhibit characteristics from multiple categories. This guide is to help assess the type of customer you are handling and adapt your strategy and communication with them more effectively. Top salespeople are adaptable and capable of recognizing and responding to the unique traits and preferences of each customer, providing a personalized and customer-centric approach to maximize sales success.

Understand Contextual and Geographical Differences

One of the key strengths needed to succeed in the sales industry relies on your ability to adapt to not just the type of customers we identified above but also various cultural and geographical traits. One of the key aspects in understanding your customer and their psychology of buying is to understand their cultural and geographical context and then adapt your approach to handle them accordingly.

Oftentimes, salespeople ignore this fact and just stick to their sales pitch, which they have been trained for and memorized. This is one aspect that even gets overlooked a lot of the time when companies are training their salespeople. The focus on the products and services overshadows the understanding of the customer, and the customer, a lot of times, just gets reduced to a 'lead' or 'prospect' who needs to be called and told the pitch. The subtle cultural and geographical nuances can have a big impact on your sales journey. One miss there can lead the customer to go cold instantly and stop responding to your calls, emails or messages.

This understanding is extremely crucial in today's global world of sales where almost all companies have offices and customers around the world. My question then is, 'why should you have the same standard approach for all customers?' This is setting up salespeople for failure from day one and leads to making 'prospects' a game of probability and numbers. The goal shifts from understanding and adapting to customers' needs to merely calling as many customers as possible and hoping to close a few by the principle of mathematical probability ONLY.

Therefore, to humanize the buying journey and not stay in the closed mindset of mathematical probability, in the section of Understanding Your Customer or UYC, I want to first address the topic of 'context' or contextual understanding of the customer. The context that I am referring to here is the cultural context with respect to the customer. Contextual understanding of your customers lays the groundwork for effective communication and interaction with them.

Lots of times, salespeople oversimplify the customer context by confusing it with geographical differences, which is not the right way to look at it. Regardless of geographical location, the principles of contextual understanding apply universally. High-context and low-context communication styles exist in various cultures around the world.

Geographical variations often compound the need for nuanced understanding, as cultural norms and preferences can vary significantly from one region to another. By establishing a foundation of contextual understanding, you will appreciate the complexities of navigating geographical differences in customer interactions and be able to adapt your approach accordingly.

So, before we dive into understanding the customer from the geographical differences perspective, the correct logical flow is to understand the cultural context of the customer first and then move on to the geographical variations.

Understanding 'Context' in Culture

Context in culture refers to the underlying circumstances, environment and social factors that shape the way people think, behave and communicate within a specific cultural setting. It provides the framework within which cultural norms, values and customs are understood and interpreted. Understanding context is crucial for effective cross-cultural communication and navigating cultural differences. In other words, it refers to the more subtle aspects of how people interact and converse.

Context can be categorized into two main types: high context and low context.

In **high-context cultures**, such as many Asian, Middle Eastern and Latin American countries, communication relies heavily on nonverbal cues, implicit meanings and shared understandings. Much of the information is implied and understood through the context of the situation and the relationship between individuals. In these cultures, indirect communication and reading between the lines are common. Customers from high-context cultures are generally collectivist, meaning they place a higher importance on the good of an entire group rather than any one individual. This stems from the fact that generally such cultures are majorly homogeneous in nature with shared commonalities, language and upbringing.

For a salesperson to effectively handle customers from a high-context culture, you will need to adapt your approach to be more **patient, empathetic and attentive.** You will generally not get direct questions and will need to probe correctly to get to understand the customer's real pain points.

Low-context cultures, including many Western and European countries, emphasize direct and explicit communication. Customers from low-context cultures tend to be demographically diverse and prefer direct and clear information flow. They tend to be more to the point when it comes to sharing their pain points and also when making decisions.

When dealing with customers from low-context cultures, salespeople should consider the following strategies to effectively engage and build rapport.

Adapting Your Approach Based on Context

For High-Context Customers

a) Establish Trust for Long-term Business

Though building trust with the customer is paramount with any customer, customers from high-context cultures put extra emphasis on this. Since this culture is highly collectivist, a good way to establish credibility is by providing reliable information, references and testimonials from other customers. Honouring commitments and following through on promises is crucial for long-term business relationships.

 With high-context culture customers, building trust and rapport is necessary before discussing business. You may have to engage in small talk or attend social events to establish a strong foundation for business interactions.

b) Be Flexible and Patient

Keep in mind that decisions and negotiations may take time in high-context cultures. You need to be patient and flexible in accommodating different cultural practices and time frames, and not rush or apply pressure, as it may damage the trust-building process.

To succeed in dealing with customers in high-context cultures, adapting your communication style is critical to match the cultural context. Using polite or indirect language and avoiding direct confrontation or disagreement is key to keeping the customer engaged with you.

Remember how we spoke about storytelling as a key skill in the previous chapters? This skill of storytelling and anecdotes to convey messages is absolutely important when dealing with high-context customers as it helps create a shared understanding.

c) Listen Actively and Adapt

Like I said before, you will need to probe to better understand the nonverbal cues from the customer, and active listening is crucial for achieving that. Pay attention to the tone, pauses and implied meanings in their speech, and listen for the underlying messages and emotions conveyed through nonverbal cues.

d) Hierarchy and Communication Style

High-context cultures often have well-defined hierarchies and roles. During your communication, you must show respect for seniority, titles and authority. For example, addressing a customer with seniority as 'sir' is preferred in comparison to addressing them on a first-name basis such as Mr John. This demonstration of humility and deference to age or position helps in communicating better with the customer.

For Low-Context Customers

a) Direct and Clear Communication

Customers from low-context cultures prefer direct and explicit communication. When dealing with them, you need to be concise and specific when explaining the benefits and value of your product or service. You should value the customer's time, especially when it comes to meetings, appointments or delivery timelines that you have committed.

Your communication style should involve focused and efficient interactions, avoiding unnecessary small talk as that can be seen by the customer as a sign of unpreparedness on the part of the salesperson. All customer queries should be handled promptly with clear timelines.

b) Facts, Data and Results

One thing that low-context customers love is tangible data and factual information that support your product benefit claims. So, use this understanding to explain to your customers with case studies, research and testimonials to back up your product's success claims. Providing examples of previous success stories and demonstrating how your offering can deliver measurable results is an effective way to keep the customer engaged and active throughout the buying journey.

> 💡 Having a strong knowledge about not just your own product but also that of the competitors for comparison and industry expertise will make the customer see you as the subject matter expert in the domain and help to build rapport and trust easily. This is called 'fostering trust through expertise'.

c) Professionalism and Transparency

With low-context customers, being transparent and open will make you look more professional. In general, these customers prefer detailed and accurate responses without sugar-coating as it helps them to make an informed choice. For example, if the customer asks you a query and you are not sure about that, the best way to handle that is by letting the customer know that you will come back on that query with details after checking, rather than giving a made-up 'unsure' answer, which can be seen right through by the customer and will make you look less professional.

Geographical Differences and Perspective

In your sales career, depending on the product or service, you would be tasked with helping customers buy—across different regions to different countries altogether. Now that you have gained a deeper understanding of the cultural context, mapping and navigating through the geographical variations and perspectives will become more logical and easier.

Dealing with customers across different geographies might seem daunting at times, but the customers you would be helping would generally lie in one of the following categories.

Domestic Customers

These are typically customers from the same country as the business or salesperson. Salespeople handling domestic customers should consider the cultural nuances within their country, such as the cultural influences specific to their country, including language, traditions and social norms. For instance, a salesperson selling traditional products in India would understand the diverse preferences across different regions and adapt their sales approach accordingly.

International Customers

These customers refer to individuals from different countries or regions around the world. Their unique cultural perspectives and expectations are critical to understanding and making the buying process smooth and fruitful. Salespeople engaging with international customers should have cultural awareness and adapt their approach to respect and align with the customs and preferences of the customer's culture. For example, a salesperson targeting customers in Japan would emphasize the importance of politeness, respect and attention to detail in their interactions.

Cross-Cultural Customers

Cross-cultural customers refer to individuals who reside in a cultural context different from their own due to migration, international education or work assignments. Their expectations and communication would generally be a blend of their native cultural background with the culture they are currently residing in. Salespeople handling such customers should demonstrate cultural sensitivity, respect for diversity, and adaptability. Recognizing and appreciating their cultural background can help the salesperson build emotional connections and trust with the customer. For instance, a salesperson understanding the preferences of a cross-cultural customer living in a foreign country might offer bilingual communication or products that cater to both cultures, thereby giving a sense of cultural adaptation to the customer when dealing with them.

Rural or Urban Customers

Rural or urban customers generally will have distinct preferences and needs based on their geographical surroundings. Salespeople catering to them should consider the unique challenges and opportunities and adapt their approach to these customers. For instance, rural customers may prioritize the robustness and reliability of a product or service more, whereas urban customers may emphasize convenience and speed when it comes to their needs and preferences. These nuances need to be considered when pitching your product or service; you will also need to prioritize those features and values in your product to the customer.

AYC The Psychology of Buying

The formal definition of the consumer psychology of buying describes it as the study of individuals, groups, or organizations and the processes they use to select, secure, use, and dispose of products, services, experiences, or ideas to satisfy needs, and the impacts that these processes have on the consumer and society.

This topic is so vast that researchers have been deep-diving into this area for decades, trying to dissect the reasons, rationale, motivation and other factors that influence the customer's decision-making process. No wonder there are many books also written on this specific topic alone.

In this book, I want to simplify it and make it easy for you to understand, enabling you to apply your understanding in helping your customers buy in a more practical way.

Let me share the framework that has always worked for me while doing this. It has given tremendous results to everyone I have coached over the years as it is very intuitive and is as applicable to you as it will be to your customer.

The framework has four basic stages of evolution, and it is important for you to understand at which stage your customer is, as that will enable you to adapt and help your customer accordingly.

> **START → SEARCH → NARROW DOWN → TRIAL/BUY**
> *(Options)*

Stage 1: START

How does the process start for the customer? It starts with a need or a desire or want to use a product or service. Generally, the customer will be the one who will start the process by identifying their needs or wants. It is interesting to note that often the challenges of cold calling customers arise from the fact that as a salesperson, you have to start the process by trying to influence the customer about a need or want on their behalf. This is also a reason why the conversion or success rates for cold calling are low at the start; instead of coming from the customer, it's coming from the salesperson.

To understand this stage of 'start', you need to understand the importance of and the difference between the needs and wants of the customer. Knowing this will give you better clarity on what to expect and approach accordingly.

Needs, simply put, are essential requirements or desires that customers seek to fulfil. They are the fundamental necessities or problems that customers aim to solve through their purchase of your product or service. Sounds obvious and simple, correct? However, needs can be further classified into two categories: functional needs and emotional needs.

Functional Needs pertain to the practical and tangible requirements or pain points that customers have. More often than not, these will be (at least should be) directly related to your service or product's core function. For instance, a customer purchasing a mobile phone may have a functional need for a device essential to stay connected with his family, friends and work, something which is critical and a necessity in today's world.

Emotional Needs are subjective and relate to the feelings, aspirations or desires that customers seek to satisfy through their purchase. Often, these needs address customers' psychological, social or self-esteem requirements. For example, buying a luxury handbag or watch may have an emotional need for the customer to feel relevant in their circle with prestige, status or personal satisfaction.

Wants, on the other hand, refer to customers' preferences or desires that go beyond their basic needs. Wants tend to be subjective in nature and will vary from one customer to the other. While wants may not be as essential as needs, they often play a crucial role in the decision-making process in the customer's mind. For instance, although a customer needs a mobile, they might have specific wants of a specific feature, colour or even brand preference that they are seeking.

The difference between needs and wants lies in their level of importance and their impact on decision-making. Needs are crucial and often non-negotiable, as customers prioritize fulfilling them to address specific problems or requirements. Wants are more discretionary and can be flexible based on personal preferences or desires. An easier way of remembering this is: needs are **must-haves** and wants are **good to have.**

As a salesperson, identifying this difference will help you understand where you need to focus with a customer and what to expect. For instance, if the start of the process with a customer is due to a want, then generally the process will either close very soon or will take a longer time. Identifying this will help you as a salesperson to set your expectations for the prospect accordingly and know exactly how to deal with such a case.

> 💡 We will see in the later chapters how to use this information in both your pitch strategy and communication technique to effectively handle the customer.

Stage 2: SEARCH

Once the customer has identified the needs or wants that they want fulfilled, they move to the next step of **searching** for available solutions. This is the step where a customer will start researching the potential products available in the market and learn more about the features and benefits.

This stage is critical for a salesperson as this gives you the best chance to captivate and engage with the customer and help them understand how your product or service fulfils their core need. During this stage, the customer evaluates and compares the most available options, their long-term and short-term benefits and how they would apply to them in solving their need or pain points. This stage is also where the perceptions that a customer has (negative or positive) about the product, brand or company come out. That is why this phase becomes absolutely critical for a salesperson to lay a strong foundation in the customer's mind for your product or service.

Stage 3: NARROW DOWN (Options)

Stage three is when the customer has, more or less, narrowed down to a few potential options that they feel fit their bill in satisfying their needs. Though the competition from other products has reduced in terms of the number of alternatives, the competition has intensified as the customer would be feeling strongly about all of them with respect to some or all features and their perceived value.

As a salesperson, in this stage, you need to focus on helping differentiate and make your product stand out in comparison to other options as the best choice for the customer. Some of the ways you can do that are by focusing on the long-term benefits of your product, producing social proof in terms of customer testimonials and reviews, and highlighting the flexible pricing options. In this stage, you need to be the subject matter expert not just for your product but also about your competitors and the market in general. Once the customer feels strongly about your expertise in the domain, they will feel much more confident in your suggestions and recommendations.

Stage 4: TRIAL or PURCHASE

If the customer is still with you on step four, then a great job is done. But it is not over yet, and there is still the last mile left to help them buy your product or service. However, keep in mind that even at this stage, the customer might still have some reservations about confidently making the purchase, so you cannot relax yet.

At this stage, your focus should be to ensure that any doubts or fears a customer may have (which you should probe properly) are mitigated. Benefits such as free trials, money-back guarantees, warranties, extensive service network, no questions asked returns, etc., are some of the ways successful salespeople use to influence the customer into buying your product.

I hope that by now you have a deep, clear and, most importantly, practical application of how to understand your customers, their types, cultural and geographical nuances, and their psychology when buying. We will be using all of this in later chapters to get more hands-on in adapting our approach when communicating, pitching and handling them overall.

Before I sum up this chapter, I do want to mention there is another important aspect of **differentiating between a customer and a consumer,** but that is something I will talk about later in the book.

Now that you have a better grasp of customer diversity, let's see how you can put this knowledge into practice. Reflect on these points, try your hand at the practices, and start planning which strategies to use.

REFLECT

- How have geographical and cultural contexts affected your sales strategies? Think of specific instances and note them down.
- Consider a recent interaction where cultural context influenced the outcome. How could you have adapted your approach now that you know more about customer context?
- How have the different customer types introduced in Chapter 2 (e.g. Digital Native, Value-Seeking) reacted to your sales approach?

PRACTISE

- Create tailored sales pitches for each type of customer mentioned in this chapter. Focus on adapting your approach based on their unique characteristics and needs.

- Conduct mock sales meetings with a colleague, role-playing different customer types that you are pitching to in your work, adapt your pitch accordingly, and ask your colleague to rate you out of five for assessment.

PLAN

- Outline a strategy with clear action points where you find yourself weak as per your reflection above. Action that strategy for the next five customer interactions and write down the assessment of it.
- Develop a training session for your team or colleagues on adapting sales techniques to different customer types and contexts. Doing this will help sharpen your understanding of the concepts.

3

Your Product and Service

Your product or service that you are pitching to a customer is the foundation or the bedrock of an effective and successful sales pitch. This is also an area which most often gets taken for granted or underplayed to just a list of 10–15 features. In my many years of experience coaching salespeople, I have often found that salespeople do not really understand the real importance of the product or service beyond the features it entails, which is why I want to focus on a dedicated chapter to highlight the importance you should give in understanding your product.

Just like we read in the previous chapter, buying psychology starts with the inherent need or a desire—from a salesperson's perspective, it is the product. One of the major mistakes I see a lot of companies training their sales force make is to have them memorize the list of features (and quite an exhaustive one) for the product, called 'product knowledge' sessions. I am afraid this is so far from the truth. I will explain to you and show you what real 'product knowledge' is, and how you should learn and approach understanding your product, which will enable you to set a strong foundation when you build your own blueprint for handling your customers.

Remember this analogy I fondly use to understand the importance of your product or service.

'If you are Messi or Ronaldo and the customer is the goal post, then your product or service is the ball. Without the ball and without knowing how to handle and dribble the ball effectively in any condition (wet, rain, dry), there is no GOAL and no WIN!'

The Real Product Knowledge

As we have done throughout the book so far, I will keep this simple and obvious so that it stays with you forever.

Real Product Knowledge will essentially always have the following three parts:

a) The type of product you are pitching
b) Value vs. features perspective of your product
c) Competitive benchmarking and industry knowledge

The Product Type

Understanding the product type refers to type of product, segment and price point you are selling at. Are you selling a luxury product, an affordable product, a mass market, a new category or an impulse-purchase product? We learned in the last chapter that when it comes to your customer, just knowing them (KYC) is not enough; rather, understanding your customer (UYC) and then adapting to your customer (AYC) is critical and important. Similarly, when it comes to the product or service you are offering to the customer, knowing and then understanding how and for which customer segment will it be useful will eventually help you to come up with the right strategies when pitching it to the customer.

Knowing and understanding your product deeply can

change your approach strategy almost 180 degrees. Let me explain this with an example.

For instance, if you are offering a product that is creating a new category on its own vs. a product in a category that is already well known to the customer and has multiple products already, your strategy will change quite substantially.

The already-existent beauty category is known to the customers, and they have been using it for a long time. Here, your focus with respect to your product will be **differentiating your product vs. the other products in the category** and convincing the customer to choose to buy your product or at least try it.

Whereas in the former case, you cannot have the same approach because in the first place, the category is non-existent or very small. So, in this case, your job as a salesperson shifts to **educating the customer about the importance of this category** and why and how it's good and relevant for them. Only after you have successfully done this can you move on to your product and talk about other aspects of the product. The product, in this case, will also help set the expectations for you as a salesperson. Not every meeting or every pitch will be sales, as you are trying to educate the customer about the category itself before pitching your product. This process will take a much longer time to convert in comparison to pre-existing categories.

Let us look at another example of two real estate agents. One is an estate agent specializing in selling properties, and the other is a rental agent. The approach of both agents will differ significantly despite being in the industry. The difference is due to the nature of the product they are offering. Someone buying a property, in most cases, is going to use a significant portion of his life savings, and that will perhaps be the only house they will ever own. The agent here will have to help the buyer with a lot of patience to ensure that the buyer feels absolutely confident in parting away with his life savings to make this purchase. It is not going to be a quick purchase and will take time. The agent will need to be a lot more patient and persistent with the customer.

The customer looking to rent a property might already be under a deadline to move out and will be quite flexible on some of the aspects of the property. It will be a much quicker decision simply because they know that the worst-case scenario for them could be mitigated with a three-month notice and lease termination. The approach by the sales agent in both cases will be significantly different based on the nature of the product they are offering.

I can give you a lot of similar examples of how effective salespeople adjust their strategies depending on the kind of product or service they are offering to the customers.

Features vs. Value

Many times, salespeople mistake the product as the sum of total features that the product has in comparison to other products in the market. But this is a fallacy that prevents many salespeople from being successful.

> Remember, customers don't buy product features; they buy the 'value' those features provide in helping fulfil their needs.

Average salespeople talk about features; good salespeople talk about the value these features provide; and great salespeople talk about the value of 'the feature', which answers the customers' primary needs 'first'.

Understanding the value of the features combined with the priority order is very crucial in ensuring you engage effectively with the customer. This understanding is used quite frequently by top marketing companies in addressing customer insights.

Back in 2004, Motorola's phone division was struggling, and they planned to launch a phone called Razr. The phone's design was like nothing available in the market. Now, if you know the mobile phone industry, you know it's a highly competitive industry. Every two months, a new phone is launched in the market, and everyone competes neck-to-neck in terms of their features, battery size, resolution, speed, memory or camera prowess. How do you then engage with the customer without losing their attention?

I am using Motorola as an example because, despite the fact that the phone was launched two decades ago, they had run a campaign where they highlighted 'one key feature' above everything else. That feature was that it was the slimmest flip phone at that time. All other features took a backseat, and their commercial ad showed a young woman struggling to wear skinny jeans but was able to slide the Moto Razr phone easily into the back pocket, highlighting the slim factor. This instantly connected with not just the male audience but also women customers like a craze, and the company beat all projections and sold over 100 million phones. The selling point was not that it was thin, but the value it added to the customer and how the value was highlighted across all marketing campaigns and sales brochures.

As a salesperson, when you are talking to a customer, always be sure to explain the value of the features of your product and explain how that value fulfils the customer's main need or pain point. The best way to do that is to put yourself in the customer's shoes and visualize how that feature would solve your needs. Needless to say, different customers might have different needs, and your engagement with the customer should always start by highlighting the value of that feature first. Let me explain this with another scenario.

Let's say you are a travelling salesman and are often out on the road for work and in back-to-back meetings. One of the key challenges you often face is that your phone battery runs dead by the middle of the day, and you start to scramble for charging stations. You walk into a mobile shop and explain your problem to the salesman. The first sales guy shows you multiple phones and starts telling you features like the phone has a 108 Megapixel camera, 12 GB RAM, Bluetooth 5.3 and 5000MaH battery. The second salesperson shows you multiple options as well and describes those options by explaining the standby duration and usage time the phone will last before needing to be charged, and then proceeds to explain other features such as speed, processor, camera, etc.

Which one fulfilled your needs? The answer is obvious. It is the second salesperson because he did two things correctly:

1. He started off by explaining the value of the features of the phone instead of just blurting out the memorized list of features of the phone.
2. More importantly, he smartly prioritized the value of the feature that will answer your pressing needs first.

These simple adaptations can mean the difference between keeping the customer engaged or losing his attention, thus losing him as a buyer.

Competitive Benchmarking and Industry Knowledge

The reason I am adding competitive benchmarking and industry knowledge as part of product knowledge is that salespeople and even the parent companies get too absorbed in only their product, making little attempt to know about their competitors or the industry expertise.

This also happens because a lot of salespeople are mistaken into believing that their job is to 'only sell the company's product' vs. 'trying to help the customer buy'. So, it is not surprising to see that this key element is either ignored or brushed away casually by salespeople under the excuse of 'our product is much better'. If you ask any top salesperson in the world, they will tell you that they know their competitors' products more intimately than some of the salespeople selling them.

You know there is a saying 'keep your friend close and your enemies closer'. I like to use a modified version of it in sales: **'Keep your product's knowledge close but your competitors' product knowledge closer.'**

A key foundation for winning the customer's trust depends on the fact that they see you as an industry expert helping them make the right informed choice for their needs. The only way that can happen successfully is if you put in the effort to learn about the latest trends and news about your industry and also your competitors. Doing this also has an additional benefit when you have to handle objections from the customer or when you need to convince the customer why and how exactly your product or service is better than the other options available.

💡 In the previous chapter, we learned about The Psychology of Buying. Expertise in competitive benchmarking and industry knowledge is critical during the Narrow Down stage in the buying cycle: Start → Search → Narrow Down → Trial/Buy

To end this chapter, I want to highlight something that I believe is the most important aspect when it comes to the product or service that you are offering to the customer.

Love your product and believe in it.

If you do not love your product or believe in it, there is no point in selling it because the customer will see right through it. Ask yourself this: if money was not a concern, would you buy your own product? If your answer is no, then do not try to offer it to the customer as it will only lead to frustration. Moreover, the customer will figure that out too and then your persistence will just become pushy.

Having covered the significance of 'real' product knowledge in sales success, it's time to test your understanding and application of these concepts through the next set of exercises.

 **REFLECT**

- Evaluate how well you currently convey the value of your product's features to different customer types outlined in Chapter 2. Focus on the customer's needs vs. your pitch on the product; what value of the feature did you start with and was that the best way to do it? Rate yourself from one to five on each of those interactions and pitches.
- Consider a few recent sales interactions. How could enhanced product knowledge have improved your persuasive ability?

Write down the areas where you feel you could have done a better job.

PRACTISE

- Prepare a detailed presentation on your product, focusing on translating features into customer benefits. This is your understanding of the product and the value; do not use the company product training deck here.
- Create a detailed comparison checklist of your own between your product and a competitor's product. Use this analysis in your next sales pitch to highlight unique benefits. Use the nearest three competitors.
- Simulate a sales scenario where you emphasize the value of a product feature over its features, incorporating the concept of 'customer-centric' from Chapter 1. Using your product knowledge, practise explaining the value of a lesser-known feature to a colleague or friend. Ask your colleague then to rate you out of five and compare that rating with the rating you gave yourself in the reflection segment above.

PLAN

- Write down three improvements or changes that you will make now that you have a better understanding of 'real product knowledge' when dealing with customers.
- Plan a monthly updates session with your product team to stay informed about new features and improvements.
- Sign up and become a user of your competitors' products to assess where they are able to handle customer needs better than your own product.

4

Your Playbook

We have now come to the part where I will help you create your own 'pitch playbook'. We will see how to use all that you have learned thus far in the previous chapters to create the playbook for you.

Your Playbook: *The Blueprint for Success*

Every successful salesperson has their own playbook that they always revisit to improvise and get better every time. Each salesperson's playbook is unique and based on their style, learning style and characteristics. What works for one may not necessarily work for another. But the basic foundational building blocks are essentially the same and all you have to do is to customize them to what works for you to become successful.

A good playbook not only gives you the right structure but also helps you self-audit and figure out where you need to improve to keep getting better. The right playbook helps you to understand and customize your approach effectively when dealing with different customers and products you are offering.

Oftentimes, I have seen amateur or novice salespeople taking the lazy approach when it comes to sales. This lazy approach is trying to put all customers in a 'one size fits all' category. There is no structure to their pitch strategy, and they try to follow the same technique with all customers and simply sell vs. helping the customer buy. Now, this may not happen by choice, but it does happen.

Let me demonstrate this with two examples: the first, where the customer approaches the salesperson to buy, and the second, where the salesperson approaches the customer to pitch a product.

Example 1: Customer wants to buy a new tennis racquet.

Salesperson: 'Hello, sir. How may I assist you today?'

Customer: 'I'm looking for a new tennis racquet.'

Salesperson: 'Sure! May I know what is the budget you are looking to buy in?'

Customer: 'I am not exactly sure. Maybe once I see, I will decide.'

Salesperson: 'No worries. Here are some of the top brands of tennis racquets, including Head, Babolat, Wilson and Yonex. All top players use racquets from these brands, but I suggest this Head racquet as it's on sale right now and is quite popular.'

Customer: 'What is the difference between them?'

Salesperson: 'Well, they are all pretty much the same as they are all top brands. But I will say Head is still the best, and like I said, it is also on sale right now. It will be the best option for you.'

Customer: (trying to lift and feel all the racquets)

Salesperson: 'Sir, take my word for it. I do this for a living.

This is the best deal you will get, and you won't be able to find a good racquet like Head at this price. Shall I pack this for you then?'

Customer: 'Well, let me have some time to think about it. Thanks for your help.'

Salesperson: 'No problem. Please let me know if you have any other questions. Have a great day.'

I am sure we all have had such experiences at some point in our lives. So, what went wrong? Let us dissect what happened here.

Salesperson: 'Hello, sir. How may I assist you today?'
(A better introduction with your name personalizes you to the customer; it is always good to put a name to a face when dealing with customers)

Customer: 'I'm looking for a new tennis racquet.'

Salesperson: 'Sure! May I know what budget you are looking to buy in?'
(Wrong approach. You can see the salesperson is asking this question to make it quicker for him to make a sale rather than focusing on helping the customer. A classic example of trying to sell versus helping the customer buy.)

Customer: 'I am not exactly sure. Maybe once I see, I will decide.'
(The customer is telling the salesperson that he is unsure, which means they may be new to this sport.)

Salesperson: 'No worries. Here are some of the top brands of tennis racquets, including Head, Babolat, Wilson and Yonex.

All top players use racquets from these brands, but I suggest this Head racquet as it's on sale right now and is quite popular.'
(The salesperson ignored probing and profiling the customer. If he is new to the sport, he may or may not know about the top brands. If he doesn't know, he will not be able to narrow down the choices, and on top of that, the salesperson, in haste to sell, simply pushes one brand just because it is on sale. Remember: mentioning sales price or discounts is used as a strategy, but it is more effective towards the later stages of the buying journey for the customer.)

Customer: 'What is the difference between them?'

Salesperson: 'Well, they are all pretty much the same as they are all top brands. But if you ask me, I will say Head is still the best, and like I said, it is also on sale right now. It will be the best option for you.'
(No attempt by the salesperson to 'help the customer buy' or to help him with his confusion about the difference between all similar-looking racquets.)

Customer: (trying to lift and feel all the racquets)
(The customer is still clearly confused and trying to figure it out himself.)

Salesperson: 'Sir, take my word for it. I do this for a living. This is the best deal you will get, and you won't be able to find a good racquet like Head at this price as we have limited stocks, and they are running out fast. Shall I pack this for you then?'
(Again, no attempt by the salesperson to actually help the customer, but rather he is trying to use the FOMO [fear of missing out] technique on the customer to create a sense of urgency for him to sell the product. Tip: FOMO is a technique

used by salespeople, but it works later in the buying journey and works more effectively when it comes to products that are generally sold as impulsive purchases. It does not work for all kinds of products.)

Customer: 'Well, let me have some time to think about it. Thanks for your help.'
(This is the customer's polite way of saying: 'thank you, but you were of no help. I will try to figure it out elsewhere.' Trust me, this customer is not coming back again. I am sure you wouldn't either.)

Salesperson: 'No problem. Please let me know if you have any other questions. Have a great day.'
(The salesperson feels like he made a great pitch, but the customer was not a genuine buyer and was just window shopping. But is he right?)

Now, let us look at another example of a salesperson calling a customer to sell an Edtech coding classes subscription.

Salesperson: 'Hi, ma'am. I am Jose calling from Great Kids Company, where Ryan took his trial class. Is this a good time to speak?'

Customer: 'Erm, I am actually about to leave for some work.'

Salesperson: 'I understand, but it will take just five minutes.'

Customer: (reluctant) 'Okay, sure.'

Salesperson: 'As you know, Ryan recently took a free trial of a coding class from Great Kids Company. So, I wanted to ask, did he enjoy the class?'

Customer: 'Hmmm, I guess so.'

Salesperson: 'That's really great to hear. I wanted to share with you more details of our coding classes and the attractive summer discount we are having for this season.'

Customer: 'Hmmm.'

Salesperson: 'We have three different packages of 24 classes, 48 classes and 96 classes where your kid will learn coding from the basics all the way to the advanced level. And as you know, in the future, everything will move to using AI. Coding is a very essential skill to learn for every kid. It will get your child ready for the future and will give him the right foundation to start with.'

Customer: 'Hmmm.'

Salesperson: 'We have a lot of kids who have benefited from our classes and are doing extremely well. And we want to share this joy with as many kids as possible. So, this summer season, we have come up with an attractive discount on all our packages. 20% discount on the 24 classes, which originally sold at $500 and will now be available for only $400; the 48 classes package, which was sold at $850, will cost you only $650; and our most successful package of 96 classes with a price of $1400 is available at a discounted price of $999 only.'

Salesperson: 'However, these discounts are only valid for the next three days, and I was wondering which package you would be interested in buying.'

Customer: 'Thanks, Jack. Let me discuss this with my husband, and I will get back to you.'

Salesperson: 'Sure, ma'am. When should I call again to confirm?'

Customer: 'I will call you on my own once I have discussed it with my husband.'

Salesperson: 'Sure, ma'am. Thank you for taking the time to speak to me. Wish you a great day ahead.'

Result: The customer never called back and even stopped responding to further calls from the salesperson.

Has this happened to you as a salesperson when speaking to a customer or have you experienced a similar conversation with a salesperson?

Now let us break up this sales pitch from the salesperson and try to understand where the salesperson went wrong.

Salesperson: 'Hi, ma'am. I am Jose calling from Great Kids Company, where Ryan took his trial class. Is this a good time to speak?'
(Good opening by introducing himself since it's a telephone call. But since it is a phone call, it is imperative and very important to have a compelling opening to get the attention of the customer.)

Customer: 'Erm, I am actually about to leave for some work.'
(The customer highlights that she is disinterested, which is quite normal for most customers when they are answering cold calls on the phone.)

Salesperson: 'I understand, but it will take just five minutes.'
(The salesperson should have understood that the opening was not engaging for the customer to give time, but he missed it and pushed for five minutes to speak.)

Customer: (reluctant) 'Okay, sure.'

Salesperson: 'As you know, Ryan recently took a free trial of a coding class from Great Kids Company. So, I wanted to ask, did he enjoy the class?'
(The salesperson wanted five minutes, but is now asking the mother to think and tell him the feedback on the class her son took. Something she may or may not be aware of or interested in telling, especially if she is busy and about to leave for some work.)

Customer: 'Hmmm, I guess so.'

(Short answers like this from customers generally indicate disinterest and the salesperson should have picked up on this.)

Salesperson: 'That's really great to hear. I wanted to share with you more details of our coding classes and the attractive summer discount we are having for this season.'
(The salesperson completely ignores the fact the customer is not engaged or interested in the current dialogue and jumps straight into explaining his product or service.)

Customer: 'Hmmm.'
(Even shorter response in this conversation. The customer is just being polite and hearing, but not listening.)

Salesperson: 'We have three different packages of 24 classes, 48 classes and 96 classes where your kid will learn coding from the basics, all the way to advanced level. And as you know, in the future, everything will move to using AI. Coding is a very essential skill to learn for every kid. It will get your child ready for the future and will give him the right foundation to start with.'

(The salesperson gets into his pre-trained format of pitching and gets into a monologue without building any connection with the customer.)

Customer: 'Hmmm.'

Salesperson: 'We have a lot of kids who have benefited from our classes and are doing extremely well. And we want to share this joy with as many kids as possible. So, this summer season, we have come up with an attractive discount on all our packages. 20% discount on the 24 classes, which originally sold at $500 and will now be available for only $400; the 48 classes package, which was sold at $850, will cost you only $650; and our most successful package of 96 classes with price of $1400 is available at a discounted price of $999 only.'

(The salesperson here is just concerned about making a sale as opposed to helping the customer buy. He just wants to get through his pitch in the same 'one size fits all' style that he has been trained in during his product knowledge session.)

Salesperson: 'However, these discounts are only valid for the next three days, and I was wondering which package you would be interested in buying.'

(The salesperson has completely ignored the art of listening to the customer and now tries to create urgency by talking about a limited-time discount on the offer.)

Customer: 'Thanks, Jack. Let me discuss this with my husband, and I will get back to you.'

(The customer politely ends the conversation by telling the salesperson she will get back, but we all know that is not what the customer is actually thinking of. And this is correct, as the customer feels this is a pushy call from a desperate salesperson.)

Salesperson: 'Sure, ma'am. When should I call again to confirm?'
(By this time, the salesperson feels he has done everything right as he was taught during his product knowledge training.)

Customer: 'I will call you on my own once I have discussed it with my husband.'
(Reaffirmation of disinterest from the customer.)

Salesperson: 'Sure, ma'am. Thank you for taking the time to speak to me. Wish you a great day ahead.'
(The salesperson feels that one successful pitch is done, and the sale can be closed during follow-up calls to the customer, but the reality is obviously very different.)

I can go through a lot of such examples of sales calls or meetings, and I am sure you would recognize some of them yourself, either as a salesperson or the customer.

It is like your dream has always been to act in the biggest arena in the world and you have worked very hard on yourself, memorized tour lines, worked on your diction, worked on yourself, but failed to deliver when you perform in front of the audience, struggling to improvise based on the audience reaction. This frustration is real and depressing. I can relate to it, and I am sure at some point in your sales career, you might have too.

That is why it is very important to have **your pitch playbook** ready. It will help you to find the root cause or gaps within your strategy with accuracy and help you to mitigate them. I will explain that as we go along and help you create your own individual pitch playbook.

Your Pitch Playbook—The 5-Block Framework

To create your playbook, we will use what I like to call the 5-block framework, where there are five main building blocks covering step by step the core foundations to help you succeed with your customer and your product. That is why it is 'Your Pitch Playbook' and not just a pitch playbook.

This 5-block framework is a culmination of spending thousands of hours coaching and even learning from some of the best salespeople I have had the pleasure of meeting and working with. This framework has helped thousands of salespeople that I have worked with, and I am confident it will help you too.

The 5-Block Framework

The framework is divided into five building blocks or stages to effectively help create your playbook.

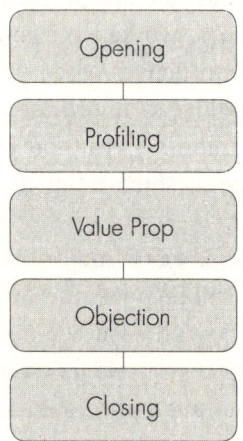

Your Opening

This is your first impression in front of the customer, whether in person, online or on the call. It's the moment where first impressions are formed and where the foundation of trust begins to take shape. Understanding the importance of crafting an impactful opening statement is paramount for salespeople striving to succeed in a competitive market landscape.

A compelling opening statement sets the tone for the entire interaction with the customer. It's the initial opportunity to capture the attention of potential customers and pique their interest in what you have to offer. A well-crafted opening statement not only grabs attention but also communicates professionalism and expertise, instilling confidence in your ability to meet the customer's needs.

Moreover, in today's dynamic market environment, where attention spans are fleeting, you must seize every opportunity to engage customers from the moment you initiate contact. To do this, make sure that your opening statement is tailored to resonate with the customer's needs, interests and pain points, demonstrating empathy and understanding. By demonstrating genuine interest and addressing the customer's concerns upfront, you can create a sense of rapport and trust with the customer, the benefits of which are a productive and mutually beneficial relationship.

Customer Profiling

This is where you apply whatever you have learned about knowing and understanding your customer in a practical context. Customer profiling enables salespeople to segment their customers effectively, allowing for more personalized and targeted interactions.

Customer profiling serves as a critical foundation block for building enduring relationships with customers. By delving deep into the intricacies of customer profiles, you can uncover unique insights that will enable you to anticipate and address the evolving needs of your customers.

Once you have **understood** your customer properly, you can **adapt** to your customer by offering tailored solutions and personalized experiences that foster trust, satisfaction and loyalty over time. In essence, effective customer profiling empowers you to forge meaningful connections with your customers, positioning yourself as a trusted advisor and partner rather than a mere salesperson.

Your Value Proposition

The value proposition here is the way you structure your product or service benefits, aligned with the customer's needs that you have probed. This section is where you apply what you've learned from the previous chapters on 'Your Product/Service' and create the best offering for the customer.

When you are handling customers in this dynamic age, one truth reigns supreme: the right value proposition for the customer. It can be the difference between making or breaking a deal. Crafting the right value proposition is not about making a sale; rather, it is about genuinely understanding what makes your product or service valuable to the customer and then effectively communicating that understanding. It's about showing the customer why exactly your product is what they need.

Picture this: you sit down with a potential customer. You have done your homework, probed well into the customer's needs and pain points, and now you are ready to offer your solution. But here's the kicker—your value proposition isn't just a laundry list of all features that your product has; rather, it's a tailored and personalized narrative that speaks directly to the customer's concerns. Whether it's saving time, cutting costs, increasing efficiency or boosting productivity, the right value proposition hits home because it's rooted in what matters most to the customer. It is like a magic key that unlocks the customer's interest, trust and, ultimately, their willingness to buy.

And let's not forget how important a customer's trust is. It not only sets you up for long-term relations but also opens the door to other customers through referrals for you.

Objection Handling

This section is dreaded by most salespeople but loved by all top salespeople around the world. If you want to be the best salesperson, you have to make this section your best friend. It is true at times that no matter how meticulously you craft your opening or probe and listen to your customer's needs, and then tailor a compelling value proposition, customers will still raise objections. This is an inevitable part of the buying journey in the customer's mind. Let me explain a bit more about this from the perspectives of the customer and also you, the salesperson.

From the customer's perspective, objections can arise due to a variety of concerns, uncertainties and priorities. Some customers might object based on price discomfort; some might feel hesitant to invest without seeing clear value in return;

and some might raise objections related to product features or functionality, questioning whether the offering truly meets their needs. Furthermore, objections may also stem from trust issues, as customers seek reassurance about the reliability and credibility of the salesperson, the product and the company to avoid buyer remorse. Sounds fair, right?

Now, from the salesperson's standpoint, objections are not to be feared but embraced as opportunities for deeper engagement and clarification. Top salespeople see objections as feedback to their pitch. They believe if a customer has objections, it can only mean one thing: the customer is interested in their product, and somewhere during their handling, they have not been able to successfully help the customer. They do not blame the customer but rather use this as feedback to make themselves better and to address the customer's concerns till they are satisfied.

In simple words, objection handling is about transforming customer scepticism into confidence and resistance into receptivity towards you and your product.

Your Closing

Just as the opening statement serves to capture the customer's attention and set the tone for the interaction, the closing serves as an equally important and pivotal moment where commitments are solidified and decisions are made. If opening is about making a strong first impression on the customer, then closing is about making a lasting impression on the customer. It's the culmination of all the hard work, relationship-building and value propositioning that has taken place throughout the buying journey with the customer.

A lot of times, salespeople mistake closing to be just a 'thank you for your time' message. Let me tell you, it is NOT. Your closing is your last chance to engage your customer into taking favourable action. And if it is a last chance, then you have to make it count and make it matter. Just like a skilled conductor leading an orchestra to a memorable crescendo, you must orchestrate your closing with finesse and precision, where all the pieces come together to create a harmonious and mutually beneficial outcome for both your customer and you.

By now, you have some idea of the purpose and importance of each of the building blocks in the 5-block framework. In the subsequent chapters, I will take you through each of these blocks or stages in detail so you have absolute clarity and confidence when using them to create your personal playbook.

You've learned how to structure your sales approach. Now, let's make these strategies actionable. The next sections will help you reflect, practise and plan your way to a more effective sales routine.

 REFLECT

- Reflect on the 5-Block Framework and rate yourself on a scale of one to five in each of those blocks, highlighting your areas of improvement for any block with a rating less than four.
- Using a recent sales interaction, reevaluate your approach using the 5-Block Framework. What could you have done differently?

 **PRACTISE**

- Conduct a peer review session where you enlist the help of a few of your colleagues to listen in or join in on your sales pitch and then rate you on the five blocks of opening to closing on a scale of one to five. Ask them to write down the reason for the rating and compare it later to your own evaluation to highlight the gaps.

 PLAN

- Prepare a fresh 'playbook' listing down the five blocks as a template. Write down the customer types and context you deal with next to it. This is going to be the skeletal blueprint, which we will start filling up as we move through the remaining chapters, so keep it dedicated as your playbook.
- Develop a plan to update your sales playbook monthly or quarterly, incorporating feedback and new learning from customer interactions and product updates.

5

Master Your Openings

As we discussed in the previous chapter, a compelling opening statement sets the tone for the entire interaction with the customer and gives you the opportunity to capture the attention of your potential customers and pique their interest. So, in this chapter, I will help you learn about the different ways to craft a strong opening that will not only grab your customer's attention but also communicate professionalism and expertise.

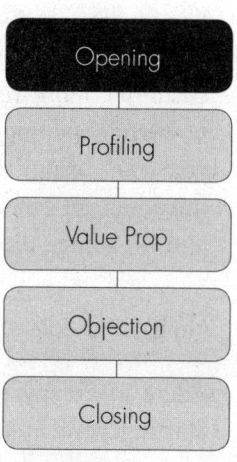

But first, I want to highlight the mistake I see a lot of salespeople make by mistaking their opening to be a mere 'self-introduction' to the customer.

YOUR OPENING ≠ JUST SELF-INTRODUCTION

Your opening is not simply introducing yourself and your company to the customer and hoping that is enough to lay a strong foundation for customer interaction. It is also logical. Imagine how many salespeople call you every day. You do not know them, and just a plain mundane opening is not enough for you to even take notice, as they will be just one of the many salespeople calling the customer every day. Don't you feel the same way when dealing with salespeople yourself?

So, always make sure that your opening is strong and compelling for the customer to take notice of you. It is like shaking the hand of a person you are meeting for the first time. The handshake should be firm and confident.

A strong opening has many benefits. It helps you demonstrate that you understand the customer's needs and challenges. This, in turn, establishes empathy, making the customer more receptive to what you have to offer. With a powerful opening, you help provide a glimpse of the value you can bring to the customer. Moreover, a compelling introduction creates a sense of curiosity, captures their interest and motivates them to engage further with you.

How to Create an Opening?

There are many ways to create a compelling opening when starting your first interaction with the customer. But instead of taking the 'hard-coded' way, let's understand it from a customer's psychology perspective. You can add your own flavour and create 'your personalized opening' that you feel comfortable with and that works for you.

When we talk about first impressions or first introductions, we are essentially talking about what emotions are invoked in the person during that interaction. If that emotion is something that the customer finds a connection with, then the first impression is successful.

Your opening should feel natural and effortless, not a memorized set of words from a script taught to you in a sales training session. Just like you, your customer will see through that memorized regurgitation of words and lose interest. Why? Because, like you, they have also heard similar scripts from many other salespeople.

How can you create an opening that is not only natural and personalized for you but also resonates with the customer when you use it? The answer to that is the customer's emotions. You must have heard often that sales are driven by the customer's emotions, and it is no different when it comes to your first introduction to the customer. Over many years of coaching and handling customers, I have been able to summarize the key emotions that customers generally respond well to and how to use them in creating an effective opening to kick-start the process of building customer engagement.

I have tried to tie up those emotions with a category of opening that you can use to help define, personalize and create your opening. The table below shows the opening category matched with the customer emotion it is intended to invoke if done properly.

Opening Category	Customer Emotion
Connection	Empathy and Rapport
Facts and Data	Trust, Surprise, Bold
Personalized	Specially 'For you'
Question	Curiosity, Excitement, Intrigue
Social Proof	Confidence, Trust, Expertise

The purpose of this table is to help you understand what emotions you are trying to invoke with a particular opening. With your understanding of the customer and their culture context, you should tailor your opening personalized for each customer.

Let's go through each of the categories and see how we can create a good opening with our customers.

Connection Opening

The connection opening uses empathy and rapport to relate to the customer or their needs. It gets the customer feeling engaged instantly since empathy is one of the best ways to make the customer feel you understand their challenges.

There are a few ways to make a good connection opening. You can use an opening that demonstrates empathy, share a personal story to build connection, use the compliment approach, or just be direct and address the customer's pain point.

Let's get practical.

a) Demonstrating Empathy

Insurance Salesperson: 'We understand that finding the right insurance plan for you and your family can be very complex and overwhelming. Let me help you find the perfect plan that will work for you and not the other way round.'

Demonstrating empathy from the outset builds trust and rapport.

Handle the customer's pain point directly!

SaaS Salesperson: 'If your goal is to generate quality that actually converts without spending a fortune on marketing, then our platform offers just that. We make money ONLY when you make money.'

b) Creating a Personal Connect

Salesperson: 'As a parent myself, I know how important our kid's health is to us. That is why we made this product, from a parent to a parent.'

OR

Salesperson: 'As a fellow entrepreneur, I know how important it is to keep costs low and still grow. Our solution is built to provide enterprise features for the entire team at the cost of only one and support your growth.'

c) The Compliment Connect

Salesperson: 'I must say, your recent product launch was just brilliant. It got me thinking of a few ways we can leverage that brilliance across all distribution channels with something as simple as a click of a button and take it to the next level.'

Facts and Data Pointers Opening

This opening utilizes facts and data and the way you bring it to the customer invokes surprise, trust and confidence in the mind of the customer. The good part of this approach is its objectivity as it stands on the foundation of facts and numbers and helps to build not just intrigue but also credibility for the product or service.

a) Use a Compelling Statistic or Fact

Salesperson: 'Research shows that when a deal fails with a customer, 91% of the time, it is due to the salesperson and

5% due to product satisfaction. We at XYZ focus on sales effectiveness to convert 91% failures to success stories.'

b) The Intriguing Data Point

Salesperson: 'Did you know that businesses using our software reported an average increase of 30% in their revenues within the first three months of usage? I'm excited to share how we can achieve similar results for your company.'

OR

Salesperson: 'Did you know that companies using our CRM software saw a 30% increase in customer retention rates, thereby reducing their overall customer acquisition cost by 20%? I'd love to show you how we can achieve similar results for your company.'

c) The Credibility Fact

Salesperson: 'We are the only company to have patented purification technology recognized in 136 countries. With over four decades of experience, all top firms trust us when it comes to purification technology.'

d) Bold Claim Opening

Salesperson: 'Are you ready to disrupt the status quo in your industry? Using our platform, you will reduce the cost of supply chain management by a minimum of 40% guaranteed. That is why we offer a 12-month, no-questions-asked money-back guarantee.'

The Personalized Opening

Personalized opening is usually used for your existing customers with an aim to provide them with a sense of exclusivity, or addressed to early adopters who would try out your product. The key to remember here is that customers need to feel valued and that your offering is customized to their preferences specifically.

a) The Exclusivity Offer

Salesperson: 'As a valued customer, I want to invite you to a sneak peek of our exclusive range, which is available to the top 1% of our patrons only.'

b) The Personalized Connection

Salesperson: 'Hi, Jake. I got to know your startup is expanding to other Asian markets. I wanted to discuss and share how your company can leverage our global footprint in logistics and help you roll out faster and with at least 15% less cost of operation than any other logistics provider.'

c) The Curated Personalization

Salesperson: 'Hi, Dea. We haven't seen you in two months and realize you must have a busy schedule and finding time for yourself can be tough. So, we have started a home service where your favourite experts, Sarah or Shane, will come at your convenience and provide the same experience in the comfort of your home.'

The Question Opening

Opening with the right question can be used to induce a multitude of emotions from the customer including curiosity, feeling of wonder, intrigue, excitement and surprise. The primary purpose of this opening is mostly to make the customer curious to know more about your product or service.

a) The Thought-Stimulating Question

Travel Salesperson: 'What if you could experience the vacation of your dreams without worrying about paying the entire expenses upfront? Where would you want to go for vacation then?'

This approach engages your audience and encourages active participation.

b) The Curiosity-Invoking Opening

Salesperson: 'Imagine waking up every morning and feeling younger and energetic. Today, I will share three simple things that can make that happen.'

OR

Salesperson: 'Imagine if there was a way to cut your internet bill in half while enjoying faster download speeds and coverage. Sounds too good to be true. Let me reveal the innovative technology that is making it possible.'

c) The Impact Question Opening

Salesperson: 'Did you know that there were approximately 800,000 cyber-attacks daily on business, making them lose an average of $3400? The potential cost of safeguarding against such attacks was only $99 per year. Protecting your business has never been more critical than it is today.'

This approach emphasizes the impact and puts it in the context of the importance of your product or service.

Social Proof Opening

This opening is used to instil confidence in the minds of the customer and highlight your product and your company as experts in the domain through success case studies, a list of existing clientele and industry recognition.

a) The Credibility Opening

Salesperson: 'I am proud to share that 85% of all Fortune 500 companies like yours trust our system as their preferred Customer Data Platform.'

b) The Success Story Opening

Salesperson: 'I would like to share a success study of a client in your industry who achieved a 50% increase in e-commerce sales after implementing our e-commerce enabler, helping them serve customers at all omnichannel touch points.'

c) The Testimonial Opening

Salesperson: 'Nothing is more satisfying than getting a call from your customer who tells you how your platform streamlined their project management process, helping them save labour costs by 15% and finish their project ahead of time.'

d) The Industry Recognition Opening

Salesperson: 'We are proud to share that our product XYZ has been voted as the 'Best Loyalty System' for the seventh consecutive year by industry leaders and clients from all industries.'

Choosing the Right Choice of Opening

The above are just a few examples of different ways you can create openings for your playbook when engaging with customers. But it is also important to understand when to use them effectively.

We learned about the **customer context** and **types of customers** in the previous chapters and will use that understanding to determine which opening might work better when dealing with specific types of customers. Another important aspect to keep in mind is the **channel of communication** you are using when engaging with the customer. In today's world, you can meet clients in various ways, from in-person meetings to a Zoom virtual meeting to a phone call. Your choice of opening in all these scenarios cannot be a one-size-fits-all approach.

For example, it is much easier for you to see the reaction

or body language of the customer in an in-person meeting, giving you a chance to adapt and make changes easily during your pitch, whereas on a phone call, you can only assume the feedback by listening to the cues while interacting with the customer.

Hence, it is generally recommended to keep your opening simple and direct when dealing with customers on the phone, and the more elaborate ones for in-person meetings so you can gauge and adapt, making it easier for the customer to understand if there are any doubts.

Also important to remember is the 'context' of the customer when using your opening. **High-context customers** generally respond well to **connection and social proof categories**, whereas **low-context customers** prefer the **Facts and Data and Question categories**. The personalized category opening is used on a much narrower group of customers; hence, it transcends all types of customers. That being said, customers move across the spectrum and the only way to master your opening is through trial and error when engaging with them and determining which opening works the best for you.

So, keep experimenting with different openings in your playbook to keep your interactions with the customer vibrant and non-monotonous. This will also help you to handle customers from different backgrounds and types more effectively, and during all of this, you will be easily able to figure out your own personalized opening that works the best for your personality and style.

After exploring various opening techniques, let's see how well you can implement these in your interactions. The exercises below are designed to help you practise and refine these techniques.

REFLECT

- Write down the different customer types and contexts you deal with for your product, and against them, write down all the opening statements you have made. Now, categorize those openings as you learned in this chapter.
- Analyze which opening techniques have been most effective with the various customer types you listed above and rate them from one to five. Why do you think some of these openings worked well?
- Additionally, rate yourself honestly from one to five on which category of opening, from connection to social proof, are you personally most comfortable with given your personality and style, five being most comfortable and one being least. The point of doing this exercise is to ensure you are building on your strengths based on your personality.

PRACTISE

- Experiment with different opening techniques in a controlled setting with your friends or colleagues and ask them to role-play different customer types and context settings. Write down their reactions post the role-play and rate yourself one to five again on the effectiveness. Now, ask your colleagues or friends to rate how they found your opening and the reason for that rating. Take that feedback to understand how your potential customers might also be reacting. Improvise with this feedback and repeat the process.
- Record yourself delivering different types of openings or even sales calls (if applicable), then review the recordings, as a third person and as the customer, to see which elements are most engaging and which elements could have done better.

Hearing your own recorded calls later is a great method as while hearing at a later time, you are able to evaluate yourself as a third person and judge better. Remember not to be biased here.

 PLAN

- Now, it's time to plan and execute what you have practised above with real customers. So, plan a rotation schedule where you focus on a different opening technique each week, tracking effectiveness and customer responses and rate its effectiveness on a scale of one to five. Wherever possible, record the interaction for more objectivity. Refine your opening techniques based on the outcomes from this and repeat the process till you have your openings rated above the minimum four for all your customer types and contexts.
- Now, standardize the most effective opening techniques into your regular pitch process, personalizing them to customer types and situations, and copy them over to 'your playbook' that you created in Chapter 4 against the block 'Opening'.

6

Your Customer Profiling and Value Proposition

What is Customer Profiling?

Customer profiling is the practical application of what we have learned in the previous chapters of 'Your Customer' and the process by which you can understand your customer deeply. As the name suggests, it is like creating a profile of who your customer is, what motivates them and what are their needs and wants.

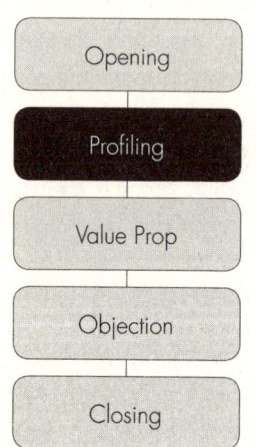

The outcome of this stage will let you understand what are the needs that the customer is looking to address and only then can you effectively customize your product's value proposition to match the customer's needs.

Apart from figuring out the needs, profiling also helps to give you a heads-up on what are some of the objections or concerns that the customer may have and, more importantly, how to mitigate these during the pitch later on.

Customer profiling is a collaborative process between

the customer and the salesperson. To do this effectively, top salespeople utilize the skill of probing.

Probing is nothing but the art of asking insightful questions that allow you to delve deeper into the customer's world and understand their specific requirements. Probing enables you to move beyond surface-level interactions and build a more meaningful and personalized connection with your customers.

> Like I said before, in sales, everything is anchored around the customer; so the deeper you 'understand your customer' (UYC), the more you will be able to personalize and tailor the solutions to 'adapt to your customer' (AYC).

A Few Proven Ways to Probe Effectively

As I mentioned above, the process of customer profiling is a collaborative process between the customer and the salesperson, and the most efficient way of doing this is to let the customer tell you. Now, I know what you must be thinking: not all customers are very forthright in telling clearly what their needs are, and you would be right in thinking so. But that is where your skills as a salesperson come into play. You need to ask the right insightful questions, which will enable the customer to open up to share their needs, fears, concerns and motivations transparently.

> The process of probing the customer is NOT TO FORCE VALIDATE what you assume to be the needs but to be OPEN to what the customer tells you and then validate it.

An amateurish mistake salespeople make is force validating their assumptions for a quick jump into pushing their product or service. This almost always leads to losing the customer and is something you should be careful about and avoid.

Picture the interaction below between a salesperson and a customer to understand what force validation is.

Salesperson: 'I can see you're a fitness enthusiast. Our elite weightlifting programme, combined with the high-intensity workout course, will challenge you to reach your fitness goals.

Customer: 'Actually, I prefer low-impact exercises and yoga for better stress management and flexibility.'

OR

Salesperson: 'I see you're interested in photography. Our high-end camera with multiple lenses will capture stunning images that will make even seasoned professionals envious.'

Customer: 'I'm actually a beginner and need a simpler camera with easy-to-use features to learn the basics.'

You can see from both the examples above that the salesperson had an assumption of what the customer's needs are and tried to force validate that. This leads to a very poor first impression for the customer and recovering from this is not easy, as the customer does not see you as someone who is trying to 'help them buy' anymore, but rather as someone who is just 'trying to sell'.

Now that you know what not to do, let's have a look at some of the ways you can make probing effective and collaborative with the customer.

a) Usage of Open-Ended Questions

Open-ended questions are a powerful tool used by top salespeople to initiate probing. They encourage your customers to provide detailed and thoughtful responses, offering valuable insights into their needs. As a salesperson, using open-ended questions allows you to gain a deeper understanding of your customers' challenges and preferences. By encouraging customers to share their thoughts and experiences, you create a more meaningful conversation and, in the process, build a good rapport with them.

Let's understand this with the help of some examples.

Salesperson selling IT software: 'Can you describe the challenges and limitations you are facing with your current Order Management System?'

(Open-ended questions like this invite the customer to explain their pain points in detail and at the same time, also what they expect from a good order management system.)

Real Estate Agent: 'What specific neighbourhoods or locations are you considering for your new home, and what factors are essential to you in making this decision?'

(This question helps the salesperson differentiate the needs from the wants and also the potential factors that can come up later in the discussion as objections. Using these insights, the salesperson can narrow down property options that match the customer's desired location, amenities and lifestyle preferences, increasing the chances of helping the customer find his perfect home.)

b) Refine Insights with Clarifying Questions

Customers may not always be clear or articulate their needs explicitly. A lot of times, the customer's initial response might be concise or vague, leaving room for misinterpretation of the actual needs or pain points of the customer. This is where clarifying questions can help uncover crucial information that will allow you to have the right insight.

Asking clarifying questions also highlights that the salesperson is listening and is genuinely interested in what the customer has to share.

Let's refine the insights from the open-ended questions we asked above and use clarification questions to probe further.

Salesperson selling IT software: 'You mentioned that your current Order Management System cannot handle orders on peak sales days. Can you elaborate on why this happens? Is it due to less system resources or due to integrations?'

(Clarifying the initial response to understand clearly as to where the actual pain point lies.)

Real Estate Agent: 'That is a great choice of neighbourhood indeed. You mentioned you have a big family; may I know how many bedrooms you are looking at on the property? Also, are there any school-going kids in the family?'

(This question helps the salesperson find the most suitable options and at the same time also figure out if having a school near the property will be necessary or important for the customer.)

c) Narrow Down the Choices Using Comparative Probing

A lot of times, your product or service might have many variants or options. In such cases, it's advisable to narrow down the choices by asking the customer their preferences and priorities among those. For that, comparative probing is the best way to determine it.

For instance:

Salesperson selling fitness classes: 'We offer both group classes and one-on-one personal training sessions. Which option do you feel would best help you achieve your fitness goals?'

Customer: 'I prefer one-on-one training as I am new to fitness and weight training and will need personalized attention and guidance to reach my fitness targets.'

(This helps the salesperson to carry on the discussion with the customer with a focus on the preferred option, thereby keeping the customer engaged.)

Real Estate Agent: 'We have properties available in different neighbourhoods—one closer to the city centre and shopping malls and another in a quieter suburb. Which location suits your lifestyle and commuting preferences better?'

Customer: 'I prefer peace and quiet, so I'm leaning more towards the property in the suburbs for my family.'

d) Understand the Customer's Emotions and Motivation through Emotional Probing

Emotional probing involves asking questions that tap a little deeper into the customer's feelings and desires. Understanding your customer's emotional needs helps to build a stronger connection to the customer and builds trust as well.

Let's see some examples for this.

Salesperson: 'Imagine other kids playing video games during the summer break and Jake learning to build mobile applications. Wouldn't that be awesome?'

Customer: 'Indeed, I agree that will be a much better investment of his summer break than just wasting time on video games.'

OR

Salesperson: 'Visualize reaching your fitness milestones and leading a healthier, more energetic life. You'd feel a sense of accomplishment and confidence.'

Customer: 'I really want to get in shape and feel more confident in my own skin. Achieving those fitness milestones would be the next level of happiness for me since I have always struggled with weight management.'

The above are a few proven ways you can probe a customer to understand their needs and use that information to customize and tailor your approach to helping the customer effectively and assisting them to buy. The examples I shared above are just a few guiding steps to give you some direction on how well-crafted probing can allow the customer to open up to you and share their real concerns or pain points. This is, in fact, the essence of when I say your job as a salesperson is not to sell but to help your customer buy. So, please work on your probing skills and invest proper effort in mastering it. This can help you deal with your customer at a much deeper level and will differentiate you from other salespeople in the eyes of the customer.

Customer vs. Consumer — *The Decision Maker*

In Chapter 2, I mentioned I would explain in detail an important aspect of understanding customer vs. consumer. Since we are talking about customer profiling, I think it's all the more important to keep in mind the right perspective about 'customer' and 'consumer'. The terms customer and consumer are often used interchangeably, but they represent different roles and relationships in the context of sales and decision-making.

As a salesperson, it's essential to understand the differences and similarities between a customer and a consumer to tailor your sales approach effectively. Both play distinct roles in the sales process, and recognizing these roles is crucial for successful results.

A customer is an individual or entity that purchases your product or services and is directly involved in the transaction. You generally encounter a customer during the buying process.

A consumer, on the other hand, is the end-user of your product or service, the person who ultimately consumes or uses it. Consumers are the individuals who benefit from the product or service and experience its features or advantages. Consumer feedback is directly aimed at your product or service and how effective it is in satisfying their needs.

Customers may have different preferences, budgets and motives for buying, while consumers have specific needs and expectations regarding the product's functionality, usage and performance. A salesperson needs to consider and satisfy both the customer and the consumer when helping them through the buying process. You may think the customer is the one taking the decision, but it may be heavily influenced by the consumer's feedback. Knowing this difference in the buying process will make sure you are answering the pain points of the right decision-maker.

Although the customer and consumer are generally different, there are times when the consumer and customer are the same person. For example, the customer buys a mobile phone for his personal use. In this case, the customer and the consumer are the same person. However, if the mobile phone is a gift for someone, then the customer and consumer will be different people.

The reason I am talking about customer and consumer is also because knowing the difference between them will make you understand who can influence the decision-making process during the buying process. Once you know that, you can adapt your approach accordingly. In certain cases, the consumer will influence the decision-making process. In certain cases it will be the customer, and in some cases, a combination of both. So be careful and assess this difference during your customer profiling to be prepared.

Crafting Your Value Proposition

By now, you have made a good compelling opening to the customer and have probed their needs and desires. Furthermore, you have gone deep into understanding the needs of the customer and the consumer, and have a rough idea of what factors might influence the decision-making process.

Now, it's time for you to make the value proposition for your product or service based on the insights that you have uncovered. We went through details in Chapter 3 on the importance of gaining real product knowledge, competitor benchmarking, and also the fact that features don't sell, but rather the value they add to customer's needs.

Building a strong and customized value proposition depending on the needs of the customer is very important to retain customer engagement. Salespeople make the common mistake of thinking that the value proposition is just telling out the features of the product to the customer.

Value proposition is NOT just talking about your product or service and its benefits, and hoping the customer will buy it. Today's customer is well informed, has researched well, and wants personalized help from you.

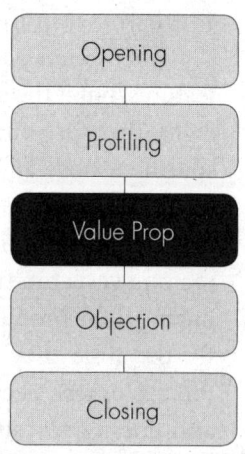

Therefore, building the right value proposition for your customer, which will actually be helpful to the customer in making an informed choice, takes a bit of effort and hard work.

Let me share with you the key elements that you should incorporate in preparing a solid value proposition based on all the information and insights you have gathered. A good value proposition will almost always have the following key elements at minimum.

Direct Mapping of Your Product Value to the Needs of the Customer

By now, you know the real needs of the customer and also the consumer, if they are different. You should map the features against those needs and highlight the value those features provide in satisfying the needs of the customer.

An important thing to remember here, which is also a mistake a lot of salespeople make, is the **order of priority** in which you map the features and their values.

For example, your product or service may have 10 great features, but if the customer need is satisfied by feature number eight, then in your value proposition, you need to map this specific feature and its value as the first feature to talk about. As a result, you retain customer engagement from the start.

Many times, I have seen the salesperson so focused on just reciting verbatim the list of features that they have memorized during their product training that the customer loses interest. By the time they reach the feature benefit that will satisfy the customer's needs, the customer has mentally switched off and doesn't pay attention. Always keep in mind the order of priority when making your value proposition, as this is what makes your proposition both personalized and customized to the customer's needs.

Quantify the Value of the Features

If you have matched the value of the features to the customer's needs in the right order of priority, then it's time to take it one step up and try to **quantify the value** these features provide when satisfying the customer's needs.

This can be a mix of hard numbers, statistics or even emotional benefits such as creating a positive customer experience that makes their life easy and happy.

For example, suppose you are selling a fitness watch. You can highlight the benefits that it tracks heart rate and sleep, which are equally essential in the body's recovery and growth of muscles, and how the customer can stay updated with just a flick of his wrist to check that. Quantifying the value of features strengthens the value of the feature and your product in the customer's mind when they are evaluating and matching these against their needs.

 This step, if executed effectively, can also be helpful in handling objections to price, as we will see in later chapters.

Comparative Analysis

Customers love to compare. Whether you like it or not, the customer, especially today's informed customer, will definitely make comparisons between products and services before settling on the final choice.

Before the customer asks, you can proactively showcase how the value of features that your product or service is providing is unmatched in comparison to the competitor products, and how your product satisfies the customer's needs completely and is better than other products on the market. This does two important things for your value proposition: 1) showcases your confidence in the product as you are willingly doing the comparative analysis on your own before being asked or nudged to do so, and 2) more importantly, the customer starts seeing you as a genuine expert who knows and understands not just their own product but also the industry and the competitors' offerings in the market.

Never say negative things outright about your competitors' products; rather, show how your product is unmatched when it comes to performance, support and, most importantly, customer service to help the customer at any time.

Social Proof

By now, the customer might be convinced of your value proposition and is actively considering purchasing your product or service. But as a customer, one fear which is very common is the fear of **regret of a bad purchase.** This is not uncommon, and neither is it illogical. After all, it is natural for anyone paying money to have this fear.

To mitigate this, you should always back up your claims with evidence, such as testimonials, case studies or success stories from satisfied customers. Social proof, such as positive reviews or endorsements, further strengthens your value proposition and provides the customer with a sense of relief against their fear of a bad purchase.

Offer to Satisfy the Customer's Wants

This part of the value proposition is what I call the **nudge over the edge.** This part, in a lot of cases, might be optional, but it is always good to keep it handy depending on the customer feedback when you are handling it.

During the customer probing step, you have uncovered the needs and wants of the customer. If you remember, needs are something 'must have' to satisfy the customer and wants are 'good to have'. Your value proposition focused from the beginning on satisfying the needs, which is the right step. In this element, you keep options to satisfy some of the wants of the customer to 'nudge him over the edge' in favour of your product or service. This is like the bonus features you provide over and above satisfying the needs. Top salespeople often use this to delight the customer and make them fall completely in love with you and your proposition.

For instance: a car salesperson will offer you four free full servicing and additional accessories with the purchase of your new car and pitch it like he is doing it 'only' for you. Let's be honest, as customers we all like that 'extra' attention and fulfilment of our wants along with our needs. So, keep this always ready to delight the customer and nudge him over to your side.

With a comprehensive understanding of customer profiling and value proposition development, let's explore how these concepts can be implemented in your daily sales practices through the exercises below.

 REFLECT

- Reflect on the last few sales pitches that you made and write down your approach on how you probed the customer needs. Now, categorize them in the respective probing technique that you learned in this chapter and rate yourself in the effectiveness of your probing skills out of five.
- In the response above, note down the points where you could have proved better or different. Take into consideration the detailed customer profiling and type (Chapter 2) and how it builds on your understanding in probing the customer's needs.
- How have your profiling efforts now improved your ability to tailor value propositions for different customers? Write down specific instances where you achieved this or where you missed it.
- Reflect on how the detailed understanding of your product or service from Chapter 3 enhanced your ability to craft compelling value propositions personalized to the customer needs. Are there any gaps in alignment?

 **PRACTISE**

- Use customer profiling to create personalized value propositions for three different customer scenarios. Role-play these with a colleague or friend. Ask them to rate you after that on a scale of one to five with reasons and feedback. Note any gaps vs. your personal rating above.
- Map a matrix of the customer types that you deal with against the most effective probing techniques that you have figured out and are comfortable with. Repeat the process until you feel comfortable with the methods and they resonate with you.
- Use the insights from your competitive benchmarking to enhance your value propositions in customer interactions.

 PLAN

- Time to go to your pitch playbook and write down the effective probing and profiling methods that work for you with respect to your customers. Develop a strategy to routinely update customer profiles based on ongoing interactions and feedback.
- Similarly, write down the value propositions that have resonated well with the customer types and context that you handle. Make a standard process for creating and revising value propositions into your sales pitch based on customer feedback to align your approach with customer needs.
- Create a monthly or quarterly review process to assess and refine your playbook with revised value propositions based on market changes and competitive dynamics and/or the addition of new consumer behaviour changes.

7

Objections—Your Friend or Foe

If there is one topic that I get asked a lot to coach on or speak about, it has to be objections and how to handle objections from customers. Some of the statements or questions I often get asked are:

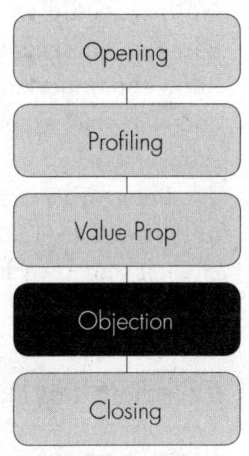

- 'I think I did everything to answer the customer's objections, yet the lead went cold.'
- 'How do I get better at objection handling?'
- 'Objection handling is my only weakness in sales.'

To be honest, if you ask a lot of salespeople, they will also have a similar perception. In the world of sales, objections can feel like roadblocks on the path to success. But I want you to take a step back and think about the next question.

> Objections: Are they really foes,
> or could they be friends in disguise?

As humans, when we don't understand something, we start getting scared of it, which leads to us disliking it and, ultimately, looking at it as our foe. It is the exact same when it comes to objections as well. When we don't understand the rationale behind a customer's objections, we start feeling daunted by it (because we don't want to lose sales), which leads us to dislike objections from customer and, ultimately, see objections as a roadblock to successful sales.

The word objection itself brings a negative connotation to the mind and sets off a defensive mindset in the salesperson. **Nothing could be further from the truth**. There is a reason why top salespeople LOVE objections from customers. They know the importance and value of objections from customers and use that as probably one of the strongest weapons in their arsenal.

Before you learn to handle something well, you need to understand it. That is what I am going to show you in this chapter and then let you decide if objections are a friend or a foe.

Objections are Indicators of Interest and Engagement

When a potential customer raises an objection, it's a clear sign that they are listening to your pitch and are engaged with you. Their objections or rather concerns are a sign of active interest in your product or service as they are trying to figure out how your service or product will add value to their needs. A non-engaged customer will not make the effort to ask any questions.

Moreover, such objections provide the perfect opportunity to engage in meaningful conversations with your potential customers. These conversations can help you get deeper insights into their pain points, challenges and desires. You can then utilize these insights to create customized solutions that truly resonate with their needs.

At times, objections are just the tip of the iceberg. While handling these objections, you can uncover deeper concerns or reservations that the customer hasn't explicitly expressed. This allows you to address these underlying issues and alleviate any hesitations they might have with respect to the value your product adds to their needs. So, embrace **objections as signs of active interest rather than obstacles.**

One More Opportunity to Bring Clarity

Objections often arise due to gaps in the customer's understanding of the value of your product or service with respect to their needs. Hence, such objections provide you with an **additional opportunity** to address these gaps and ensure that the customer has a clear and accurate perception of the value of your product or service. This clarity paves the way for a more informed decision-making process.

This process of clarification not only helps the customer to understand your product better but also helps you to fine-tune your pitch. Repeated clarity-seeking questions on a particular feature will give you an idea of where to spend more time when explaining your product to a new customer.

Strengthens Trust and Your Credibility

As we discussed before, customers often buy into the salesperson before they buy the product. This trust is very crucial for every salesperson to build with the customer as it makes the difference between getting a customer to put his ink on the paper and closing the deal or not. So, when customers see that you're genuinely interested in addressing their concerns, it builds trust and credibility. This trust is a vital foundation for nurturing long-lasting customer relationships.

Top salespeople understand that objections often stem from scepticism, doubt or simply a misunderstanding. They see this as an opportunity to transform this doubt or misunderstanding into trust by showing genuine empathy, skillfully addressing all the objections and finding the right solution for the customer. This helps the salesperson not only build a strong rapport and trust with the customer but also makes the customer see the salesperson as a genuine expert who is trying to help him buy instead of just rushing him to close the deal for his own interest.

It is no wonder that top salespeople, instead of fearing objections, embrace these as friends because they recognize the insights, opportunities and relationships that objections can bring. They embrace objections as they see it as an opportunity to get to know their customers better, improve their own skills, and, ultimately, help more and more customers to buy with peace of mind.

Objection is a Strong Precursor to Closing More Deals

Effectively handling objections in sales is a vital step towards closing more deals. It acts as a trust-building mechanism between the prospect and the salesperson.

Objections are the customer's way of giving the salesperson another chance to clarify and reinforce the value that their product or service adds to the prospect's needs. It helps to showcase a genuine commitment by the salesperson to understanding the customer's needs and concerns and working with them to find the best customized solution for them. Remember, prospects are always more inclined to do business with individuals they trust.

It is very logical for any customer, who is the one who will pay for the service, to have a lot of objections. No one wants to part with their hard-earned money unless they feel absolutely sure about it. No customer wants to have buyer's remorse, and it is, therefore, all the more important for the salesperson to help the customer feel more confident in their purchase. Through handling objections effectively, the salesperson can identify and address the specific concerns or misconceptions that may be hindering a prospect's decision-making process. By actively listening and providing thoughtful responses, salespeople can remove those barriers and fears from the prospect's mind and make them feel more confident about proceeding with a purchase.

Objection Handling is NOT Just about Countering Objections

Rather, it is about incorporating a holistic approach by fostering meaningful dialogue with your prospect, empathizing with the concerns and fears they have, both verbal and nonverbal, and then using your expertise to create tailored solutions for them. This not only enhances the chances of closing deals but also lays the foundation for enduring customer relationships.

In summary, remember this mantra about objection handling that is followed by all successful salespeople the world over:

> The more objections a customer raises, the more
> are the chances of him buying from you.

Communication during Objection Handling

Before we delve into the details of objections and how to handle them, I want to mention some successful tips for communicating with the prospect while you are handling their objections. It is important to pay attention to this part as a lot depends on how you communicate to the customer while handling their objections, which will help them understand and see your point and explanations in the right way.

Some of the key successful strategies that all top salespeople incorporate during their communication with prospects while handling objections are:

a) The Art of Active Listening

You must have heard this many times: listening is a very important skill in the arsenal of successful salespeople. The art of active listening is paramount when handling objections as it enables you to clearly understand for yourself the real concerns the prospect has in his mind regarding your product or service. Until you understand correctly what the concern is, it is impossible for you to frame your response in a thoughtful and relevant way for the prospect.

Remember, when you were pitching the values of your product or service, you did your bit of talking and the prospect was listening. Now, it is your turn to listen properly before you start speaking.

Doing so helps you to:

i) Probe the real objection that the customer is facing,
ii) Identify any nonverbal concerns that the customer might be facing,
iii) Show respect to the customer by demonstrating your genuine intent in listening to them rather than just jumping to sell your product.

b) Empathize by Acknowledge, Assure and Answer (AAA)

One of the best ways to build a rapport with the customer is by showing empathy towards their objections and concerns. The only way to do that effectively is by trying to put yourself in their shoes and understand where their concerns are coming from.

You can do this effectively by using the AAA method of **Acknowledge, Assure and Answer** with the customer's objection.

Acknowledging objections demonstrates respect for the prospect's concerns and validates their perspective. It conveys to the prospect that their opinions and questions are valued, fostering a positive and respectful interaction.

Assuring the prospect is crucial because it helps to take away any apprehensions they might have, making them more forthcoming in sharing their concerns with you. It's essential to reassure them that their concerns are valid and that you are committed to addressing them.

Lastly, **answering** objections with well-thought-out and relevant responses is the core of objection handling. Since you've shown empathy in understanding the customer's objections and assured them of your commitment to address them, the customer becomes more open to listening intently to your explanation, further reinforcing trust and credibility.

For example, if a prospect raises an objection about the reliability of a product, acknowledging their concern, assuring them of the product's quality through warranty or testimonials, and then providing specific data on product reliability would be an effective objection-handling strategy. These steps collectively ensure that the prospect feels heard, valued and well-informed, increasing the chances of a successful sales conversion.

c) Answer with the Positive Affirmation Method

One of the biggest mistakes a rookie salesperson makes is to quickly jump to negate the objection raised by the prospect. Starting an objection response with a 'no' can be counterproductive in sales as it creates a negative and confrontational tone that might escalate the objection rather than resolve it. Keep in mind that when a prospect raises a concern, they are often looking for reassurance or information. Responding with a flat 'no' or any negative tone will be perceived as dismissive and destroy the rapport with the customer.

Furthermore, responding or starting with a negation will shut down the conversation with the customer, and they may not be willing to explore or share their concerns with you anymore. Objections often carry underlying reasons or unspoken concerns that need to be uncovered through further dialogue. Responding negatively from the outset can hinder your ability to understand the prospect's perspective fully.

Lastly, remember that your job is not to sell but rather to help the customer buy. Your job as a salesperson is to provide solutions and address concerns to meet the prospect's needs. By starting with a 'negative word', you close that opportunity to position your product or service as a viable solution to their objections. Instead, it's more effective to begin objection handling with a positive and solution-oriented approach that shows your commitment to addressing the prospect's concerns.

For example, if the customer has raised concerns or fears about the features of your product or quality, and you know they are probably generalizing or have completely missed the part of your pitch where you had specifically spoken about the five-star quality rating of your product or service, instead of losing patience and jumping in haste to tell the customer they are wrong, try the following approach.

Salesperson: 'I see where you're coming from, and I would agree that this is a valid fear or concern, especially given the fact that most other customers raised a similar concern regarding products in this category. And this is exactly the reason why we are the only company that offers a no-questions-asked full money-back guarantee for six months. The only reason we are able to offer that is because we are the only five-star rated product in the market, which is certified by three international quality assurance agencies.'

This type of response reassures the customer that you understand where they are coming from, that you are empathizing and giving your response to tackle that objection. It makes the customer more open to listening to your point of view, which, in this case, is your second opportunity to tell the customer about the value of your product or service that they might have missed out on during your pitch.

d) Honest and Transparent

Honesty and transparency are paramount when you are handling objections from prospects. Your transparency and honest approach signal to the prospect that they are dealing with someone who can be relied upon. Trust is especially crucial in high-stakes sales where significant investments or long-term commitments are involved.

It also adds to your credibility as someone who has the prospect's interest as a priority over just closing a sale. When a salesperson provides accurate information and openly addresses objections, they establish themselves as knowledgeable and trustworthy experts in their field. This credibility goes a long way in positioning the salesperson as a reliable source of information.

Most importantly, it is essential for any salesperson to set realistic expectations when dealing with the prospect. It's better to be upfront about the limitations or challenges of a product or service rather than oversell it and risk disappointing the customer later. Managing expectations honestly ensures that the prospect knows exactly what they are getting, reducing the chances of post-purchase dissatisfaction and, thereby, their trust in you.

e) It's Not Personal

A common mistake that I have seen being made by a lot of salespeople during objection handling is they take it personally. It is important that you understand that objections are not personal attacks on the salesperson; they are simply expressions of the prospect's concerns, needs or questions about your product or service. Understanding this fundamental distinction allows the salesperson to remain composed and professional in their response. Taking objections personally leads to the salesperson getting defensive, which leads to nothing but damaging the rapport and trust built with the prospect and eventually losing the deal.

The moment you take it personally, you lose the perspective of actively listening to the prospect's concerns and needs. Rather, you start focusing on preparing your response, which may not necessarily address the prospect's concerns or objections. This also takes the salesperson away from their core responsibility, which is to help the customer buy. Keep in mind your main responsibility is finding the best solutions to meet the prospect's needs, not defending your ego. This customer-centric approach is a key driver of successful objection handling and builds a positive impression of the salesperson as a problem solver rather than someone who takes things personally.

Understanding objections is crucial, but mastering them requires practice. Move on to the next sections to reflect, practise and plan how to turn objections into opportunities.

 REFLECT

- Reflect and write down three words or phrases that first come to your mind when thinking about objections. Now, after going through the chapter, how many of those feelings still seem justified?
- Reflect on a time when addressing an objection effectively led to a successful sale and a time when the sale fell apart. How did your approach in both cases differ based on what

you learned in the chapter? What were the turning points in both the approaches and, specifically, what could you have done differently in the second approach to turn it into a successful outcome?

 PRACTISE

- List down the common objections you encounter from your current customers and practise responding using the AAA (Acknowledge, Assure, Answer) approach.
- Role-play with a colleague or friend and ask them to portray different types of customers and raise objections over different categories. Record the new objections that are different from the common ones you've recorded above.

 PLAN

- Record and listen to your sales pitches to customers and note strictly how many times you did not practise active listening and jumped to cut the customer to make your point. Improve your active listening skills till the number of interruptions during the customer talk becomes zero.
- In your playbook, make a tracking sheet for objections you face from customers, categorizing them by customer type, objection type (leave it blank as this will be used in the next chapter), and your response effectiveness.

8

Making Objections Your Best Friend

Now that we are all on the same page about objections being, in fact, friends in disguise, let me make a bold claim unanimously agreed upon by all top salespeople worldwide.

Objections are a salesperson's best friend!

This is where true professionals stand out from the rest. If you want to be a top salesperson, you need to master the art of handling objections and make it your best friend.

Logical vs. Emotional Friend (Objections)

As you navigate the world of sales and dealing with customers, you'll inevitably encounter a myriad of objections. From my extensive experience dealing with countless objections across diverse clientele, it's become clear that these objections fall into two distinct camps: logical and emotional.

Think of it like your friends with varying personalities; some are driven by reason, while others are guided by their emotions. As a salesperson, recognizing and understanding these distinctions is paramount. It's this ability to discern between logical and emotional objections that empowers you to effectively address the multifaceted concerns and hesitations that customers may encounter along their buying journey. So, let us get to know these friends a little better.

a) Logical Objections

These are objections that stem from a rational analysis of the product or service that you are pitching to the prospect. These objections often relate to specific facts, features or practical considerations. For example, a prospect might raise a logical objection regarding the price, citing that it exceeds their budget. In this case, the objection is grounded in a straightforward evaluation of affordability, making it a logical objection.

b) Emotional Objections

These are objections that are driven by feelings, perceptions, fears or subjective judgements. They are less about the cold, hard facts and more about the prospect's emotional response to the offer. For instance, a prospect might express a fear of change when considering a new software system for their business. This fear is an emotional objection rooted in the discomfort associated with adopting something new and disrupting existing routines.

It is important to understand the distinction between them, because knowing this will help you to understand and prepare you to handle them effectively with your prospect.

For example, logical objections can often be resolved by providing additional information, redemonstrating the value of your product or service, or offering solutions like discounts or payment plans. Handling emotional objections will require you to show empathy and understanding. Sales professionals need to listen actively, acknowledge the prospect's feelings and help them overcome their emotional barriers through reassurance, storytelling and building trust. Typically, the AAA method that I explained above comes in very handy in handling emotional objections.

Now that you have understood the distinction in the broad categorization of objections in general, let's go through a method I've taught many salespeople. It's a method that has proven quite effective. I would like to call this MT. CUSP.

MT. CUSP stands for:

M – **M**oney or Price Objections
T – **T**rust & Credibility Objections
CU – **CU**stomer Fears and Concerns
SP – **S**ervice or **P**roduct Objections

MT. CUSP

Most objections that you will hear from the prospects will fall into the subcategories mentioned in MT. CUSP. As we go along in the chapter, I will take you through various examples and how top salespeople have used MT. CUSP to handle almost any objection with ease.

I would like to mention here that objection handling is like solving a math problem. There are many ways to reach the same solution, but the fundamental basics of math will remain the same. Similarly, you will realize that as you handle more and more prospects, you will start to adapt and give your own unique twist to MT. CUSP and the ways to handle the objections. However, the fundamental basics of MT. CUSP will remain the same.

So, as a salesperson, your focus should be to climb MT. CUSP successfully, as that is when you will reach your goal of helping the customer buy and close the sale.

MT. CUSP—Money or Price Objections

Objections regarding price are one of the most common objections you will face in your sales career. It is natural human behaviour to raise objections, especially when they are the ones paying for the service or product. There it is very important for you, as the salesperson, to understand each unique rationale the customers are driven by while raising the objections. Once you know the root cause of that objection, you will be far better placed to address and guide the prospect toward a positive buying decision.

Let us look at some of the common reasons why customers raise price objections and their underlying rationales and, most importantly, what strategy you should focus on to effectively handle them and help the prospect.

a) Budget Constraints

One of the most straightforward reasons for price objections is that the customer's budget simply doesn't align with the price you are proposing for your product. They may genuinely like the product or service but find it financially challenging to commit to buying it. Their primary concern is whether your product or service will fit within their budget limitations. Their rationale is purely guided by the aim of ensuring they are making a responsible financial decision.

Although easy to understand and accept, often customers may not be very forthcoming about their budget constraints. This is where you will have to use your probing skills effectively, as we learned in previous chapters, to figure out the real cause for raising the price objection. Once you have figured that out, you can move on to helping them with your proposal addressing the objection.

Strategy to handle: Since you know that the objection is logical and a genuine constraint, your strategy should be around offering flexible payment options or discounts to fit your product or service in the customer's budget. For example, instead of charging an annual fee, you can offer quarterly payments or even a monthly subscription plan, making it more affordable for the customer.

Let us apply the strategy to some real-world objections from customers.

Customer: 'I'm interested in your software solution, but it seems a bit expensive for my small business budget.'

Salesperson: 'I completely understand your budget constraints. Many small businesses face this challenge. Let me do something and create a tiered pricing package to suit your needs. Instead of an upfront annual fee, would you be comfortable with quarterly payments or monthly payments?'

Customer: 'I think quarterly payments would make more sense given our budget constraints. Thank you.'

How about another example?

Customer: 'To be honest, I love this designer handbag, but it's quite pricey and beyond my budget, unfortunately. Maybe I will come back in a few weeks to pick it up.'

Salesperson: 'I understand your budget concerns. But as you know, our brand sells out quickly, and this bag may not be available in a few weeks. I might be able to help you as we do have a financing option available, so you can spread the cost over 12-24 months as per your convenience, making it more affordable, and you can walk out today with your favourite bag. All I would need is your ID to start the process.'

> 💡 See how the salesperson started the response by acknowledging and empathizing with the customer's objection before proceeding to offer the tailor-made solution, which makes the customer more open to listening to the salesperson.

b) Perceived Mismatch of Value

Price objections are often raised by customers when they feel that the value provided by the service or the product is not sufficient to justify the price demanded. Their rationale is based on a perceived imbalance between what they will receive and what they will pay. This mismatch between perceived value and cost makes the customer uncomfortable about making the decision. One of the key reasons for this mismatch in the mind of the customer is that they may not fully comprehend the impact of the product or service to their core needs.

The salesperson's strategy to handle price objections raised due to the perceived lack of value by the customer should be to emphasize the value added by the benefits and features of the product to the customer's core needs.

For example, a car salesperson will often have to deal with such objections.

Customer: 'This car is no doubt spacious and comfortable, but company X has a similar model with almost similar features and is cheaper than this model. They are both family sedans, so I don't know why there is such a price difference.'

Salesperson: 'Sir, that's a valid concern. Our cars are indeed priced a little higher than cars from company X and let me explain to you why. Apart from our build quality, which is the best in the sedan class, your purchase comes with a comprehensive warranty, which includes free maintenance for three years. It ensures peace of mind and adds significant value compared to other options. Company X will charge you an additional amount for a comprehensive warranty, which, if you add up, will actually cost you more than what I am offering.'

> A lot of times, during your pitch, a customer may not remember all the value and features that you explain. Hence, as a salesperson, it becomes imperative for you to show patience and help the customer, closing any gaps in understanding.

c) Price Comparison Objection

It is quite normal nowadays for customers to have done their own research by the time you approach them. Customers love to engage in comparative shopping, evaluating similar products or services from different providers. If they have found a competing product or service offer that appears to provide a better deal, they will raise the objection to you in the desire to secure the best value for their money.

Remember, there is a slight difference between the **perceived mismatch in value** and the **price comparison objection**. In the former objection, the customer has either misunderstood or completely missed some of the key tangible values of your product or service. In the latter objection, it is more of the intangible value and benefits that your product provides that you have to make the customer aware of while handling the objection.

Let me explain this subtle difference with an example for better clarity.

Customer: 'I've seen other property listings with the same built-up area, number of bedrooms and amenities but with lower prices. Why is this property more expensive?'

Salesperson: 'I understand you've been looking, and you are right about the lower prices for such properties. But the reason this property is priced slightly higher is that it includes energy-efficient upgrades, a sought-after school district within walking distance of five minutes, a supermarket and a well-established neighbourhood. Since you have a family with young kids, I am sure these factors will make it not only convenient for them but also safe and provide you with peace of mind. These valuable features actually make the price for this property reasonable given the long-term value they bring.'

d) Negotiation Tactic

Some customers raise price objections as part of a **negotiation tactic with the hope of getting a discount or concession.** They may not necessarily have budget constraints but believe that by objecting to the price, they can secure a better deal from the salesperson. The good part of this objection is that you know the customer is interested and it's just a matter of smart negotiation that brings a win-win situation for both the customer and the salesperson. The onus of this is with the salesperson to make it happen.

The strategy to keep in mind here is to be prepared to negotiate with the customer while maintaining the value of your product or service.

Here is an example explaining how.

Customer: 'My wife and I really love this vacation package, but the price seems a bit high. Can you offer a better deal?'

Salesperson: 'You have chosen the best vacation package; however, due to the high demand for this package, it is not really possible to give an additional discount as the deal I have offered is already the best price available. However, let's see what we can do. How about I include an extra night at the resort and a spa credit at no additional cost, making this an even better value for your wife and yourself to create more memories together.'

e) Sticker Shock

Sometimes, the customer may raise price objections due to something called a **sticker shocker**. The sheer size of the price tag can trigger an initial surprise or shock as the customer may not have fully anticipated the cost or was not prepared for it. The customer usually gets taken aback by the big price tag, and the knee-jerk reaction is to raise the price objection.

The strategy to handle such objections is to **work with the customer and break down the big price tag** into smaller, more manageable components and prioritize them on the basis of immediate relevance to the customer's needs.

One of my salespeople working in a B2B company used this strategy while handling the sticker shock objection from a customer due to the heavy price tag of the software service.

Customer: 'The price of your software is simply overwhelming and is nowhere near my budget. Your product is more suited to large conglomerate groups rather than our SME company.'

My Salesperson: 'I agree, the total price of the software may seem very high, but it is simply because it contains around 12 modules covering everything from procurement and order management to logistics and warehouse management. However, you will not be needing all the modules, so why don't we write down the key modules that you will need for the size of your business right now? As your business scales up, you can add more modules. That way, you will still get the benefit of a world-class software, but you'll only pay for what you use.'

The salesperson eventually closed the deal with the SME customer starting with just one module, which made it within the customer's budget and as months went by and the business of the customer scaled up, he eventually used eight modules of the same system.

This same strategy is used by many companies and salespeople across industries to calm the customer's initial shock into a more manageable and acceptable situation.

Picture this: you would have seen salespeople or companies marketing their prices by mentioning 'you only pay for what you use', or the strategy being used in the telecom world when 'per second' billing was introduced instead of block billing.

f) Affordability Concerns

A common mistake rookie salespeople make is to confuse **affordability concerns with budget constraints**. They sound similar, but they are very different when you empathize from the customer's point of view.

Budget constraints happen when a customer's financial plan or allocated budget for a specific purchase is limited or fixed. In other words, the customer may have a predetermined amount set that they are willing to spend on a product or service. On the other hand, affordability constraints refer to a customer's broader financial capacity to make a purchase, considering their overall financial situation. It's not just tied to a predetermined budget but considers whether the purchase is affordable within their financial means.

Now that you understand the difference between budget and affordability concerns, your strategy to handle this and help the customer would go beyond flexible payment plans to offer viable financing options or lower-tier alternatives to your product or service to bring the purchase within financial prudence for the customer.

Some salespeople that I have seen during my career miss out on offering the 'lite' or 'lower-tier' version to the customer as they are thinking of the commission from the sales of the 'high-tier' version of their product. But again, like I have been saying, your primary responsibility is to help the customer buy.

MT. CUSP—Trust and Credibility Objections

Customers often raise trust objections when considering a product or service, and these objections can be attributed to various reasons. Trust here can refer to the customer's trust in the brand or the company, the product or service being offered and, more importantly, the salesperson himself or herself. The rationale for these trust concerns in the minds of customers can be due to a lot of factors, including past experience or the current information they have received during the pitch by the salesperson. Understanding these objections and having effective strategies to address them is crucial for successful sales.

Below are several reasons why customers raise trust objections and the rationale behind each, along with strategies on how to handle them.

a) Lack of Credibility in the Brand

If you are a new company or brand in the market, customers may question the credibility of the product or the brand as they may question the quality and reliability of the brand and, thereby, its service or product. Trust can be fragile in such situations, and thus, the salesperson needs to be careful to mitigate this concern, as without building trust, the conversation with the customer will not yield any fruitful conclusion.

Strategy to handle: The salesperson should establish the credibility of their company or product through third-party endorsements, such as customer reviews, industry awards or certifications. Sharing success stories or customer testimonials helps to showcase your company and product in a positive light, helping to mitigate the credibility concern.

Let's go through an example of how a salesperson handles an objection for a new supplement product company.

Customer: 'There are new supplements coming out every day and most of them eventually end up being scams just conning customers out of their money. To be honest, I do not know if your products are genuine or not.'

Salesperson: 'We share your concern, and you are right there have been a lot of scams going around in the market for supplements. Let me show you one of the easiest ways you, as a customer, can verify that yourself. Genuine companies like us spend a lot of time getting FDA approval before launching the product in the market, whereas others launch it while pending FDA approval. Moreover, we source our ingredients from certified suppliers, and every product batch undergoes rigorous quality testing, as you can see in this test report. And our biggest proof are our long-time customers, and here's feedback from one of them: "I've been using their supplements for years, and I always feel confident about their quality and authenticity."'

b) Negative Experiences in the Past

When customers have **unfavourable experiences** with either your brand or product in the past or similar products, services or companies, they may harbour scepticism and lingering doubts or mistrust due to unsatisfactory encounters with similar offerings and just want to ensure they don't repeat those experiences.

The effective way to handle such concerns is to first acknowledge past issues (if they happened with your company or product) and then provide evidence of improvements or changes that have been made to ensure the same does not happen again. However, if the negative experience the customer had was with a similar offering or company, then take time to showcase clearly how your company and product value differ from those of the competitor and back that up with customer testimonials to strengthen your statement.

Let's handle a customer who has had some bad experiences with your products earlier and reassure him.

Customer: 'I've heard mixed reviews about the reliability of your products. Your price is attractive, but I am wondering how this will be any different from your other products?'

Salesperson: 'I understand your concern, and to be honest, we have had some issues with our previous products indeed. To fix this permanently, we now get our chipsets manufactured locally in the country to ensure tighter control over the quality standards. Our brand has been at the forefront of technology for years, and customer satisfaction is of paramount importance to us. That's why this laptop comes with a five-year warranty instead of the market-standard two-year warranty. Additionally, we have a dedicated support team available 24/7 now to answer any of your queries. Because of this, we've received high ratings for this particular range of laptops on performance and reliability from independent tech reviewers, which you can check online as well.'

c) Post-Purchase Support

The **fear of inadequate customer support** can deter customers. Customers believe the salesperson will sell the product or service, and then if the customer needs assistance or support, they will not be able to get adequate help and support if any issues arise. This is also prominent if your company is new or not well recognized, or if it has negative reviews on customer support online.

The strategy to handle this is to first assure the customer that your company has a dedicated customer support setup, and most importantly, you, as the salesperson, will always be in touch or can be contacted if there is any issue with the product or service needing support.

 We will cover this important aspect again in detail in the later chapter on Customer Service.

Now, let's take an example of this!

Customer: 'I've heard horror stories about car dealerships not providing good service once the sale is done and that the customer is left out on his own to handle all the issues himself. Since I am buying this car for my wife, I do not want any such hassle.'

Salesperson: 'Being there in the industry, I will be honest with you. Unfortunately, such dealerships do exist and bring a bad name to the genuine ones. However, let me assure you we value our customers even after the sale, which is proven by our long tenure in the business and strong referral base of customers. Our service centre is renowned for its expertise, professionalism and efficiency. We value not just your business but also the referral business you will be giving us as a satisfied customer. Here's a customer's recent experience: "I had an unexpected issue with my car, and the dealership not only fixed it promptly but also provided a loaner vehicle so I wouldn't be inconvenienced."

Moreover, even after the purchase is done, I will always be one call away for any help that you would need.'

d) Ambiguous Claims and Unclear Information

At times, during the pitching of the product or service, the salesperson gets excited about explaining the product or feature's benefits without showing evidence. This creates **ambiguity in the customer's mind**, and they start doubting the product claims, believing them to be vague or exaggerated.

This objection is easy to handle by providing the customer with verifiable evidence and straightforward information, especially on the results that are your product's unique selling points (USP) and set you apart from the competition. This will not only help build trust in your product but also subtly justify the price point of your product or service for the customer.

A recent company that I was consulting for had the following as one of the major objections to their sales team and this is one way we handled it successfully.

Customer: 'I love organic products, but they are generally expensive. How is it that you claim your products to be truly organic and yet at this price? It just doesn't add up as genuine in my head.'

Salesperson: 'This is one of the most asked questions from customers about our products. Let me explain why we are able to offer this price and yet keep our products 100% organic and genuine. Other brands source their ingredients from third parties, which increases their price and provides no control over the quality. However, we grow our ingredients on our own farms, maintaining the quality control and authenticity of our product. Our product is the only one certified by XX, one of the most respected organic certifiers. We also maintain complete transparency about our sourcing. This is the reason why other brands list their ingredients on the back in small fonts, while we print them in bold on the front of our label. In fact, you can visit our farms anytime and see for yourself our dedication to authenticity.'

e) Trust in the Salesperson

As I mentioned before in the book, **customers usually buy into you as the salesperson first, before buying into your company or product**. This happens when they feel the salesperson has their interest first and is genuinely interested in helping them with their needs. This rapport is strengthened or weakened by the salesperson's expertise in the domain and market insights.

Ideally, this situation should not arise as this should be the basis for every salesperson who wants to be successful in sales. As a salesperson, you need to ensure you actively listen to the customer's needs, go the extra mile in addressing their concerns, build rapport and establish a personal connection with them, show genuine interest in their needs, and highlight your expertise and experience by tailoring a customized solution for the customer to strengthen that trust.

Let us explore this with an example of what happens in the financial industry.

Customer: 'I want to invest, but I've heard about financial advisors giving biased advice or poor advice due to lack of experience. How can I trust you'll have my best interests at heart?'

Salesperson: 'I appreciate your concern. Trust is the cornerstone of our advisory practice. Since we operate on a fee-only model instead of a commission, it means our sole focus is to ensure that we cater to your best interests only. It is in our interest to provide you with unbiased, objective advice tailored to your financial goals. Moreover, I have been in the industry for over 12 years and my clients' investment portfolio ranges anywhere from $5,000 to over a million. This trust from my clients shows I understand their goals and then tailor the solutions to fulfil their goals. I am proud to say that my clients have seen substantial growth in their investments and have consistently praised my commitment to their financial well-being. If interested, I will put you in touch with a few of them to validate my claims and way of working.'

f) Lack of Guarantees

Customers often **seek guarantees or warranties as a form of insurance** against potential dissatisfaction. This also differentiates the product from the competitors and often adds credibility to the product's quality as it ensures the company's trust in their product's claim of benefit delivery and, more importantly, the aspect of reliability of the product. When such assurances are absent or unclear, they may raise trust objections.

So, as a salesperson, you need to mention this upfront and, if required, re-emphasize the guarantee and warranty aspect of your product as it helps to alleviate any doubts the customer may have regarding the reliability of your offering.

Below is a great example of how to handle such objections.

Customer: 'All electronics products are now OEM, made by cheaper companies. They break often and then there is no way to fix it. I've had this experience multiple times now, so how is your product any different?'

Salesperson: 'We understand your concern, and you are right in the experiences you have shared. However, our product will change that perception for you as we offer not just a manufacturer warranty of three years but also give you an extended two-year warranty with our product. It means you will have peace of mind for an additional two years even after the manufacturer's warranty ends. There is no other company in the market that is confident in their product quality to offer this to their customers. We value the customer's happiness and peace of mind over extra margins.'

MT. CUSP—Customer Fears and Concerns

Customers' fears and concerns often get disclosed in the form of objections towards the salesperson. These objections can be influenced by a range of emotions, past experiences or anxieties. Since often these objections might come from the 'emotional objection' angle, the salesperson will have to be patient and handle this delicately with the customer and help alleviate the concerns.

You will have to take more of a consultative approach while handling these kinds of objections and help the customer feel at ease with respect to those fears and concerns, for them to move forward with your proposal.

Let me help you explain some of the common customer fears and concerns and how to handle them effectively and help the customer along the way in their purchase journey.

a) Buyer's Remorse

This is the most common form of fear anyone buying wants to avoid. Even you and I will not want to be in a situation where we purchase something, and it doesn't work out correctly and we are left feeling frustrated or stupid for making that decision. This is why a lot of customers often hesitate because they fear making the wrong decision, especially when purchasing high-value products or services. This fear is rooted in the worry that their choice might not meet their needs or expectations, leading to regret.

Handling Strategy: To address this fear effectively, salespeople must adopt a consultative approach (which we studied in the previous chapters) and thoroughly understand the customer's needs, preferences and pain points. Apart from identifying and tailoring a solution that addresses their needs and pain points, you have to go a step forward and provide assurance to the customers that they can change their minds if the product doesn't meet or address their needs effectively, by offering a satisfaction guarantee or easy return policy.

Let me show you how I worked with the sales team at an Edtech company in Latin America with a new product for kids. Since a product like that had not existed in the market before, it was bound to have objections and hesitations from the parents.

Customer: 'The product right now seems good, and I am sure it will add value, but I am afraid my son might lose interest soon and then I will end up paying for something without any use and then regret this purchase.'

Salesperson: 'I understand your concern and the hesitation, and you are right. Kids generally have a short attention span. But the reason why our product works so well for kids all around the world is that we make learning the most complex topic fun by gamifying the lessons and assignments that kids love. Moreover, I am confident that your son will love our classes. To ease your worries, I will offer you a 30-day satisfaction guarantee. You can try it risk-free, and if it doesn't meet your expectations, we'll provide a full refund with no questions asked in 48 hours.'

b) Fear of Financial Risk

Customers raise objections when they feel concerned about the financial implications of their purchase. The rationale behind this fear is that customers worry about hidden costs or unexpected expenses. The unexpected expenses can be in the form of maintenance or upkeep costs for the product or service, which increases the fear of extending the burden on the customer's budget in the future.

The handling strategy for such objections will generally require the salesperson to **provide transparent pricing, break down all costs and explain them**. At the same time, they should offer any financing options, if applicable. Moreover, the salesperson should explain the long-term value for the customer and validate it by showcasing case studies and testimonials from other customers that will demonstrate how the purchase will benefit the customer financially over time.

Let us understand this better with an example.

Customer: 'I like the car and the pricing, but I'm worried about the long-term costs of maintaining this car model. This is making me think if I should not be ambitious and rather go with a smaller car that will be more suitable for the long run.'

Salesperson: 'Your concern is valid. However, if you would allow me, I want to show you why this model is the best suited for your needs in the short run and, even more so, in the long run. This model has a strong track record of reliability and fuel efficiency of a minimum of 15% over any other model in the same category. In addition to that, our customers report, on average, lower maintenance costs compared to other brands. We are also the only brand to offer an extended warranty package that covers major repairs for up to five years. If you take all that into consideration, I am sure you will see why in the long run too, this model will be the best selection for your family.

If you want, I would be happy to put you in touch with some of our happy customers of this model so you can make the decision with peace of mind.'

c) Fear of Uncertainty

Customers may raise objections due to fear of uncertainty about how the product works or if it will meet their expectations. The key point to remember here is not that the customer doesn't believe that the product works, but rather he is more concerned about whether the product will work for him and deliver the same great results as claimed or as experienced by other customers.

The best way to handle this objection with the customer is to offer them product demos or, even better, a fully functional trial to play with your product and service. **Providing demos**

or trials lets the customer explore the value of your product or service hands-on and get a feel for how the product fits into their life and solves their needs.

Let us help a customer with their multimedia cloud software over bulky existing software.

Customer: 'I like what I see, and I can see the benefits of your cloud multimedia software giving me the freedom to work from anywhere with just an internet connection, but I am not sure it will be able to do all the things that I need for my more complicated assignments.'

Salesperson: 'I see your hesitation, and the only way to satisfy it is by letting you experience the power of our award-winning cloud software. Let me set up a live demonstration and provide you with a 30-day fully functional trial where you can explore the features hands-on. You'll get a better feel for how our product fits into your daily life, handling the most complicated tasks with ease. Like they say, seeing is believing. At our company, we say experiencing is believing.'

d) Concerns about Commitment

No one likes long-term commitments unless they are very sure of what they are getting into. Isn't this true for everything we do in life? So, why would it be any different if you became a customer?

The fear of commitment is a customer objection rooted in the apprehension of making a long-term commitment to a product or service. Customers often hesitate when they perceive a purchase as binding or inflexible, especially when it involves contracts or subscriptions.

Luckily, there is a proven way to handle this objection effectively. To do so, the salesperson should focus on emphasizing the flexibility and value that comes with the purchase of their product or service. You can do that by offering flexible payment plans, trials and the option to cancel or return the purchase without penalties.

Once the customer is convinced of the value your product adds to their needs, then highlight the benefits of a long-term commitment, such as cost savings or member-only advanced features that will demonstrate the value in committing. Customers who are generally happy with the product prefer to have long-term contracts as they do not like to keep going through the cycle over and over again. Your goal is to ensure the customer gets to experience this love for your product or service and help them get over this fear of commitment.

A classic example of this—one that you must have experienced in your daily lives and has now become almost second nature—is subscribing to telecom contracts.

Most of us have taken some sort of telecom subscription contract for one or two years as it comes with a lot of benefits, such as getting the latest smartphone for a significantly reduced upfront cost and unlimited data. Couple that with a 30-day trial period where you can cancel without any penalties.

e) Inertia to Change

The inertia to change is a common customer objection that arises when individuals are hesitant to adopt a new product or service because of the fear associated with the disruption of their existing practices and routines. The rationale in the customer's mind for this is the discomfort that is associated with the potential challenges and unknown challenges that will come as part of a new implementation.

Ask anyone who is into B2B sales, and he will tell you how frequent and important this objection is, and till you resolve this objection, nothing will move forward. This is also a reason why the deal closure times for B2B sales are significantly longer.

The only way to handle this objection successfully is to address this fear of change by highlighting how the benefits of the new product or service will add tangible value to their system—for example, improve efficiency, provide significant cost savings, enhance productivity, or automate redundant tasks. More importantly, highlight that the same will be implemented in phases to minimize any disruption to the business. Follow this up with extensive handholding, training and support for all during the transition so the customer does not feel left on his own to figure things out.

Let me share an example of one of my friends who deals in B2B sales and had to close a deal for a supply chain and logistics solution, which had been stuck for a few months. The customer, despite understanding the value of this transition, was not moving toward execution due to multiple factors and stakeholders. The CTO had concerns about the implementation complexity and whether his team would be able to utilize it successfully. The CFO also had concerns about the billing since the project could take some time to complete while incurring bills towards both the existing vendor and the new vendor. Lastly, the CBO was concerned about the impact on business operations, thereby affecting the top line of the business.

Here is how we worked to resolve all of these objections and successfully helped the customer.

My Friend (Salesperson): 'I understand that this project is complex in nature and hence your concern. However, let me break down the implementation strategy that we have utilized for multiple clients and effectively implemented the solution.

Since our software is designed in modules, we will do the implementation in four phases so there is minimal impact on your business. During the entire duration of implementation, our technical team will be posted here, at your office, and will work with your team to ensure nothing gets missed during implementation.

Furthermore, your teams will be comprehensively trained by our system experts and handheld till they are comfortable with the new processes. Also, our support team is available 24/7 during the transition phase to ensure a smooth changeover.

Lastly, I want to mention that the license billing for the software will only start once the entire implementation is successfully done so you don't have to incur double costs to two vendors. I hope this reflects our commitment to your business and our partnership.'

The deal was officially signed five days later.

MT. CUSP—Service or Product Objections

Customer objections around the product or service you're offering generally come either because there is a **gap in understanding by the customer** or he or she needs more clarity to determine if the product will actually address their needs in their specific context.

The objections around the product or service can be many, a reason why we had gone through a dedicated chapter on

'Your Product/Service' earlier. It is quite natural to have a lot of objections or concerns around your product or service—these are inevitable aspects of any sales deal and you need to have a hands-on approach as, at the end of the day, that is what you want the customer to purchase.

Customers can raise objections about the product or service in terms of its **quality, capability, competitors, complexity of implementation, extent of customization, future updates, warranty, customer support, ROI in the long term and, more importantly, the actual need for the product.**

Since we have gone through some of these reasons, such as quality, capability, competitor's offering and customer support, in Chapter 3, we will cover the other common objections that customers raise when it comes to the product or service and how to handle them successfully.

a) Product Need

Customers may genuinely like your product or service but are unaware of its benefits or the problems it can solve for them. They like what you show them but are unable to ascertain exactly how it will add value to their existing lifestyles and needs.

Now, logically, you may think that if the customer himself does not feel he needs it, then what is the point of pitching it to the customer? **But often, customers need to be shown what they need before they realize they need it.** And this is where top salespeople show their skills in making the customer see what they have been missing without the product. The probing skills of the salesperson play a crucial role in engaging with the customer and showcasing how the product or service will bring tangible value to them.

Let me demonstrate this with an example from the e-commerce industry.

Customer: 'I like the service you are showing me, and it does make a lot of sense, but I am not sure how it will add value to our existing e-commerce setup as we already use an expensive CRM system to reach out to our customer through emails and WhatsApp.'

Salesperson: 'I understand your concern, but let me show you how our system will add value to your customers and thereby add value to your business with increased sales. The current CRM systems do send emails and WhatsApp, but they do so in bulk and all at the same time when set up manually in the system at a scheduled time. As you know, different customers behave differently, and the right nudge at the right time can mean the difference between the customer acting on it or ignoring it. This is what our system does; it sends each customer personalized communication at the right time, thereby increasing the probability of the customer taking action to make the purchase on your website. The best part, it is all done automatically with no intervention as our system learns the customer behaviour on your website and takes action.

All our customers have reported a minimum increase of sales of 23% post implementation of our solution.'

b) Customization

Customers love testimonials and reviews from other satisfied customers, but they do tend to be different in terms of their needs and wants. This requires customization and flexibility for the product or service to adapt to different scenarios and still deliver results.

Let us continue the discussion with our customer above and see how to handle his customization objection.

Customer: 'Ah, I see now what you mean, and definitely the right nudge at the right time is absolutely important when it comes to a purchase decision. However, we just set up our CRM system last year and have three more years to contract with them, so changing the entire system is not feasible at this time. Moreover, we prefer to use SMS instead of WhatsApp messages, to be less intrusive to our customers.'

Salesperson: 'I am glad to see we are on the same page when it comes to delighting customers and I do understand your concern about having spent a significant amount of money on the existing CRM system. However, to use our system, you will not need to change or replace any existing systems; in fact, our system can sit on top of your existing CRM system with just one API integration and do its work flawlessly. Regarding communication channels, we offer multiple communication channels from WhatsApp, email, SMS and other popular providers and they are as easy as clicking a button to enable or disable as per your needs.'

c) Future Upgrades

Depending on the type of product or service you might be offering a customer, they may raise objections regarding its lifecycle and future support in terms of upgrades or updates. These objections are very common for technical products or services.

Our customer above is listening to you intently but now is concerned about the future upgrades and complexity and multiple system upgrades.

Customer: 'That is good to hear that your system does not need to replace any of our existing systems, but how will you guys handle updates or upgrades when our existing systems go for upgrades?'

Salesperson: 'That is a very valid point indeed that lots of customers miss out on. As I told you, our system is built to deliver over a simple browser, so any upgrades or updates to your existing systems will not have any impact on our solution. Moreover, since we are browser-based, any new updates or features that we will add to our solution will be immediately available for you to use at no extra cost.'

d) Long-term ROI

This objection is raised by the customer because he wants to ensure he is getting more than what he is spending on your product over the entire lifecycle of your product or service. This is a great objection to have as this implies the customer is already doing the numbers in his mind to justify purchasing your product, and this is where he needs you to step in and show that to him.

Our customer above is almost convinced, but he knows he needs to finally get an okay from his finance head as implementing your system is going to be an additional cost. So, let us help him justify the long-term ROI of our product or service.

Customer: 'I am convinced by whatever you are saying, but at the end of the day, we are a business and implementing your solution will be an additional cost to our setup, and I am wondering if it is going to be worth it.'

Salesperson: 'I agree with your concern, and I am happy to tell you that over 90% of our customers have broken even on their investment in our solution in the first three months, and the remaining 10% in the first six months. I did some numbers to show you a rough calculation, and if you use our system, we are able to provide incremental sales of only 11%. The investment in our solution will break even in two and a half months for you. Furthermore, to sweeten the deal, we won't charge you for the first month for you to see the results yourself.'

Now that you have learned how to climb MT-CUSP successfully, it is time to reach the pinnacle and hoist your flag—or in our words, mark the final stage of helping the customer and closing the deal. In the next chapter, we will learn some of the time-tested and proven closing techniques that you can personalize to your way to help the customer buy. But before we go to the next chapter, I will suggest investing some time in going through the assignments below across Reflect, Practise and Plan so you have not only firmed up the concepts but also applied them practically.

Having explored advanced techniques for turning objections into advantages, let's now deepen your understanding and skills and transition from theory to practice with the next set of exercises, which will challenge you to apply and enhance the objection-handling strategies discussed.

REFLECT

- On the list of all objections that you prepared in the assignment of the previous chapter, make two columns, the first being emotional/logical objection and the second being the category of MT. CUSP it belongs to.
- Analyze a few sales interactions that you had, and record the objections raised and how you responded to them. Now categorize those objections in the relevant category of MT. CUSP and reflect on how your approach to these objections can be improved or evolved based on what you have learned in Chapters 7 and 8.

PRACTISE

- In the list of objections created in the first assignment reflected above, it's time to add the relevant handling techniques against those objections and role-play with your friends or colleagues. I would suggest trying different approaches to the objections while role-playing. Now, ask your colleague to rate your handling skills out of five and give feedback on the reason for the rating. This process will help you with two key realizations—firstly, you will know which ways of objection handling you are most comfortable with basis your personality, and secondly, practising it enough times will give you confidence when handling customers of different types and contexts. Remember, this assignment needs to be an exhaustive attempt and not a touch-and-go.

Making Objections Your Best Friend

 PLAN

- We are back to your playbook. Create a matrix there that maps objection types to handling strategies that have proven effective from your detailed practice exercise above. Craft your personalized handling statements to the common objections and make them a reference guide to quickly look up in your playbook.
- Establish a monthly review process to assess and refine objection-handling tactics based on new sales insights or objections from customer handling and feedback.

9

Sharpen Your Closing Skills

Closing—the final act in the grand performance of sales—is both an art and a science, requiring finesse, patience and undaunted determination. This is the moment when all the stars align, rapport is built, objections are addressed, and the value proposition presented to the customer converges into a resounding 'yes'. It is the culmination of countless hours of your hard work, perseverance and preparation bearing fruit. It is that last quarter mile in a derby race where you can see the finish line and glory beyond it.

'Top salespeople are great deal closers!' I am sure you have heard of this statement sometime in your career. In fact, a lot of companies have experienced salespeople who specialize only in deal closing. Their experience built over the years with thousands of customers makes them the top gun in the industry, and they are brought in to help close the deal.

I am sure by now you are convinced of the importance of closing skills and are wondering what you can do to master this art.

Before I answer how to master the art of closing, I want to first clarify what closing is. Of course, there is a definition meaning of closing and then there is the real meaning when it comes to sales.

Closing skills in sales are the strategies and techniques

employed by salespeople to persuade a prospect or customer to make a purchase and finalize the sale. But what does it mean in simple terms? What are you trying to achieve? Just to make the sale?

The answer is no. Closing isn't just about pushing products or persuading customers. It's about forging meaningful connections with them, understanding their needs and delivering value that resonates deeply with them. It's about navigating the twists and turns of their buying journey with finesse and confidence, guiding them towards a resounding 'yes' with grace and skill.

I have seen countless sales deals go wrong when salespeople get impatient or resort to using an 'xyz' closing technique and jumping to the sales question. Remember, we are not trying to sell but to help the customer buy.

If you have reached this far with your customer—probing and understanding their needs and handling their objections effectively and climbing MT. CUSP—then you need to be patient and have the same customer centricity in the final leg of the buying journey with the customer.

Another important aspect in closing is to understand that it is the process of helping and guiding your customer to the 'next logical step' in their buying journey. Now, this could be signing the sales contract, yes, but before that happens, it could also mean scheduling a demo session, a site meeting or even a planned follow-up. Understanding this distinction is crucial for any salesperson as each of these little logical steps will take you towards closing the deal.

Now, let's see how you can master the art of closing. The only way to do that is by understanding this natural progression and the next logical step based on the customer's response or reaction and adapting to it, fine-tuning your approach and continuing to help the customer buy. It is like when you go for dinner at a nice fine-dining restaurant. You always begin with the starters or appetizers, followed by the main course, the salad course, and you end the dinner with a nice dessert. You don't jump to the dessert but patiently go through all the courses before enjoying the dessert.

But here comes the next challenge and, in fact, a pertinent question I get asked by salespeople: how do I know which closing technique to use with the customer?

It is a valid question as there are more than a hundred closing techniques that I can mention, and I am sure you can find even more than that if you read other literature on sales. Unfortunately, closing techniques are not a magic wand (even though every salesperson would wish they were), and no one will be able to tell you exactly which technique to use to 100% success. But then, this is what separates the top salespeople from the rookies. This art of closing gets mastered with experience of dealing with thousands of customers during your career. Also, not all closing techniques that you will learn will be applicable to all customers uniformly.

> Remember the chapter on the customer; their types and context play a pivotal role in determining which closing will resonate more with the customer. For example, a direct close approach may work well with a customer from a low-context culture, whereas the same approach with a customer from a high-context culture will almost surely result in the customer getting cold.

But that doesn't mean you are left to figure out how to navigate through these hundreds of closing techniques on your own. In fact, this is one of the biggest pitfalls in a salesperson's career when they memorize the closing methods and try to apply them without understanding the right context of their customer.

In this chapter, I will take you through a structured and logical framework of closing skills and explain the principle at each step so you are able to figure out with better accuracy where you are with your customer in his buying journey and what should be done.

The 5-Step Framework for Closing

The 5-step framework of closing is merely a logical sequence that the customer might be in or move through as you assist him. I just want you to take care of these steps and remember them while serving your customers. Once you can correctly understand what step your customer is at, it will be simple for you to know what kind of closing technique to use without memorizing all of them. Remember that you can only help your client make meaningful decisions if you are aware of what stage in his buying journey he is currently at.

Step 1—Recap and Confirm

The first step is generally where most customers will be when you are in the initial stage of closing. Once you have handled all the objections from the customer effectively, you **should recap the entire conversation** and indirectly help the customer realize that you have handled all the concerns the customer had and that the product or service you are pitching addresses the customer's needs completely.

Think of this step as a lawyer making his closing statement, summarizing all that happened during the trial and indirectly proving how his client's case stands better. This step helps to bring the customer to the same page as you, and if the customer still has any initial doubts, you can handle them promptly and then guide the customer to further steps.

> Whenever you are in doubt or have trouble figuring out at what stage the customer is, it is a good idea to start your closing from step 1.

Step 2 — Testing with Trial Close

Once you have done a successful recap and confirmation, it is always good to **test how warm the customer is for purchase** by doing a trial close. A trial close is an indirect way of checking the pulse of the customer and how ready he is to make the purchase.

If you get a positive response from the customer in this stage, then you can easily move to stage four or even stage five from here. However, if you sense a little hesitation or reservation still from the customer, then you have to move to step 3 in the framework.

Step 3 — Probing Customer Hesitation

If you sense customer hesitation during step 2, it is important to address it properly as doing any other thing or employing just any closing technique would come across as a forced sell jeopardizing all the hard work, trust and rapport that you have built with the customer so far.

This is where you have to use your probing skills again to understand where exactly the customer hesitation is stemming from and handle it accordingly before moving to steps 4 and 5.

What I have seen is that customer hesitation comes broadly from the following three categories, which, once identified, can be then addressed for the customer. Customer hesitation at this step will mostly be about:

1. Like the product but do not feel the urgency
2. The product value, price, or both
3. Concerns about risk associated with the purchase

Once you have successfully probed the hidden objection behind the hesitation, you can tailor your response to help the customer overcome that.

Step 4—One Step Closer

I call this step 'one step closer' because this one entails getting the customer the final surety about the purchase before they will have to buy the product or service. After successfully going through step 3 above and helping the customer overcome the hesitation, this step is critical in getting the customer a glimpse of owning the product and making the commitment.

This step is a critical piece in the jigsaw puzzle of closing and needs to be handled carefully and with tactical precision. It is the last effort to reassure clients that their decision counts, before they finally decide to make an order for a particular product or service.

Step 5—Go for It!

This is the **finish line or the pinnacle of MT. CUSP**—the step where you ask the customer to sign the deal and complete the purchase, or, in other words, dot the i's and cross the t's and get it signed, sealed and delivered. This is where the customer shakes your hand and says, 'It's a deal!'

I have made this 5-step framework for closing with two prime objectives in mind—to make it easier and to make it relevant for you as a salesperson. Understanding this will enable you to know which particular closing technique at which step of the buying journey **helps you to help the customer**.

Let us now get into the details of some of the time-tested and proven closing techniques that can be used effectively in each of the five steps in the framework described above.

Step 1: Recap and Confirm — Closing Techniques

a) The Summary Close

The Summary Close technique is a powerful method used by some of the most successful salespeople. It is used to **reiterate and emphasize the key points of the sales pitch** by summarizing the benefits, features and, more importantly, the value of the product or service and reminding the customer of what they stand to gain by making the purchase. The principle behind the summary close technique is rooted in **the psychology of memory and persuasion**. People tend to remember information better when it's repeated or summarized. Therefore, by summarizing effectively, the salesperson refreshes the customer's memory and thereby increases the likelihood of positively influencing the customer's buying decision.

For example, a salesperson selling SaaS marketing services can utilize this summary closing as follows.

Salesperson: 'So, Dave, let me recap our marketing services. Our solution will help increase your brand's online visibility, generate four times leads, and ultimately grow your revenue. To add to that, our AI-driven data analytics will provide valuable insights that will help to create personalized targeting and offers for your customers, aiding in better conversion rates. Did I miss addressing anything?'

The reinforcement of how your product or service addresses all the needs of the customers often prompts the customer to make a positive buying decision because they've been reminded of the benefits and advantages of the offer.

b) The Framing Close

The Framing Close technique is a great persuasive technique based on the idea that people are **influenced by how information is presented to them**. By framing the value of your product or service positively and addressing potential objections proactively, the salesperson can influence the customer's perception and make the offer more appealing. It leverages the principles of cognitive psychology, where perspectives can be influenced based on the context and the way the information is framed. Successful salespeople use this technique to shape how customers perceive their offer, by presenting it in a particular context or frame.

The Framing Close technique is quite effective because it helps guide the customer's thinking and decision-making process and enhances the value perception of your product or service.

Let's see it in action with an example of a salesperson helping a customer with a travel vacation package.

Salesperson: 'John, I understand you might be concerned about the cost of this vacation package. However, if you consider that it includes accommodation at a five-star resort, all meals included and all activities with a reliable local tourist guide, it's actually a fantastic deal. Our loyal customers find it more cost-effective than planning everything individually. More importantly, you won't have to worry about the hassle of arranging anything on the vacation but focus on creating incredible memories with your family. Isn't that precious?'

In this example, you can see the salesperson proactively addressing potential objections by framing the value of his product in a way that emphasizes its value and benefits and takes it further by making the customer visualize himself enjoying those benefits with his family. This technique helps steer the customer's perception toward a more positive view of the offer, making them more likely to agree to the sale.

Step 2: Testing with Trial Closing Method

Now that you have recapped and summarized effectively, we will go through some of the proven closing methods to test the waters with the customer to see how ready they are for a favourable purchase decision.

a) The Assumptive Close

The Assumptive Close technique, as the name suggests, is based on the principle that you, as the salesperson, assume throughout the conversation that the customer has already made the decision to purchase your product or service. While **assuming the agreement on the customer's behalf, you're**

nudging them to either confirm their decision and validate your assumption or provide objections that they may still have, which you can then proceed to handle and take the conversation forward.

This method of closing is quite effective because by assuming their agreement, it creates a subtle sense of obligation in the mind of the customer. This technique is particularly useful when you believe that your customer is favourably leaning towards a positive decision but might need a little push to seal the deal.

Personally, I have used this method a lot during sales transactions.

Real Estate Salesperson: 'Based on what you've told me, this house seems like an ideal fit for your family. It is spacious, has schools nearby for your kids, and the safe and friendly neighbourhood makes it perfect. Your family would be happy, and a happy family makes a happy man. So, should we discuss the down payment and closing date?'

The same method for an insurance salesperson would look like this.

Insurance Salesperson: 'Rob, given your priority on your family's well-being and future financial security, our insurance plan provides the most comprehensive coverage with 24/7 support anytime you need it. All this at the lowest premium in the market. From what date do you want the insurance to start? Next week or from today itself?'

The Assumptive Close doesn't pressure the customer but gently guides them towards a positive response. It's important to use this technique when you've built rapport, addressed objections and detected buying signals. However, if the customer still has objections, this approach will encourage them to voice their concerns, allowing you to address them effectively and then go for closing.

b) The Choice or Alternative Close

The Choice or Alternative Close is based on the principle of offering the customer a **choice between two or more options, all of which lead to a positive outcome for the salesperson**. As I said before, anyone who is paying wants to feel that he made the decision to buy, and not someone selling it to them. Therefore, framing the decision as a choice rather than a simple yes or no makes the customer feel empowered and gives them a sense of control in the buying process.

It also makes you look good in front of the customer as you come across as a salesperson who genuinely wants to help and someone who respects their autonomy and preferences, making the customer feel valued and listened to.

You can employ Choice Close in almost any sales deal across any product or service. For example:

Retail Clothing Salesperson: 'Madam, you couldn't have picked a better dress than this for the occasion. Would you prefer this dress in black or red or shall I pack them both?'

Hospitality Salesperson: 'Our Executive Chef has prepared two exquisite signature dishes tonight: a succulent steak in Balinese spicy sauce and a savoury risotto with sautéed mushrooms. Which one would you like to enjoy?'

Software Salesperson: 'You can either select our monthly subscription, which offers flexibility for your monthly budget limit, or you can go for the annual subscription, which comes with a significant cost-saving upfront. Which payment option works better for you?'

In these examples, you can see clearly that the salesperson avoids a simple 'yes' or 'no' response by presenting alternatives that cater to different preferences or needs. The Alternative Close technique guides the customer to decide while still maintaining a positive feeling throughout the interaction.

When using this closing technique, **always ensure that both presented alternatives are appealing**, making it more likely for the customer to choose one and move forward with the purchase.

c) The Indirect Close

Some customers are resistant to a direct sales pitch and react better to a **more subtle approach**. This is where the Indirect Close works better. It helps by subtly guiding customers towards a purchase decision without directly asking for it. This method is quite effective because it feels less confrontational and allows the salesperson to persuade customers in a non-pushy manner. This approach generally works well with **customers from high-context cultures** as it is subtle and not very direct.

Moreover, this way also helps elicit more genuine responses from customers as they don't feel pressured. Instead, they believe they are deciding independently, thereby giving the customer the autonomy of decision-making, which can lead to a higher likelihood of closing the sale.

The Indirect Close puts the customer at ease vs. the pressure of giving you an answer which, as per statistics, has a 70% chance of leading to a negative answer.

Let us understand this approach and how to use it effectively with the customer.

Car Salesperson: 'I think you would have explored a lot of options today, and that is great. From my experience, people often find it helpful to take a few brochures home and discuss their choices with family. Why don't I prepare some information for you along with a test drive so you can take your family along and feel the difference between our model and others and then make the decision?'

Financial Services Salesperson: 'I can see that you're overwhelmed with a lot of information, and this is normal when having to choose between options, especially when it concerns your financial future. Many people choose to consult with a financial advisor before making a commitment. Would you like me to schedule an appointment with one of our experts who will be able to help you?'

Here, the salesperson subtly guides the customer towards the next step, whether it's taking materials home and booking a test drive, or consulting with an expert. The Indirect Close respects the customer's need for time and consideration while gently moving them closer to a purchase decision.

Remember, closing is not always about making the customer buy immediately. Your core goal should always be to help the customer buy and help them patiently along their buying journey.

d) The Contract or Direct Close

Sometimes, when dealing with the customer, you might get strong positive 'feelers' about the direction the conversation is going toward. Or, as they say in some cultures, 'the iron is hot'. One of the best approaches to test this is using the Contract Close. It involves presenting the customer with a contract or written agreement, outlining the terms of the purchase and inviting them to sign or commit. By doing so, you emphasize the seriousness of the offer and encourage the customer to act. This approach also helps as it reduces ambiguity and clearly defines the terms of the deal. It creates a sense of finality and commitment and encourages the customer to commit.

However, it is important to remember that **the Contract Close should typically be tried when you feel strongly that the customer** is happy with your pitch and handling of all his objections, and feels your product or service addresses his needs. If used at the wrong time, it can make you look like a pushy salesperson who is only interested in getting the sales done and does not respect the customer's concerns.

Look at the examples below to understand the difference and effective time of using this approach.

Customer (looking for home renovation): 'Looking through your extensive portfolio of work and the way you have explained all the little nuances, I am confident you guys might be what we were looking for.'

Salesperson: 'That is great to hear and indeed we have handled projects like yours successfully in the past. By the way, based on what we have been discussing on your exact requirements, I have prepared a contract detailing the scope of work, materials and complete project timeline. Once you review and sign it, we can start transforming your vision for your place into a reality.'

Real Estate Customer: 'Of all the options that I have seen so far, this one looks the best fit for my family and also budget. I've been looking for a place like this for a long time.'

Salesperson: 'You are absolutely right; this area is highly sought after by customers with families especially. That's why I have already prepared the contract for the property with complete details on the terms, price and any contingencies that we've discussed. If you're ready, we can sign it now and make this your "home sweet home".'

The beauty of the contract closing if used at the right time is it provides clarity, transparency and a clear path to the customer to closing the deal.

Step 3: Probing Customer Hesitation— The Closing Approaches

Going through step 2 above will let you know exactly where your customer is during the buying journey. If he seems a little hesitant while you are trying the different closing approaches, it signifies the customer still has some objections or concerns regarding the purchase of your product or service, and this needs to be handled promptly.

As I mentioned before, customer hesitation post step 2 generally is about the following three broad categories:

1. Like the product but do not feel the urgency
2. The product value, price, or both
3. Concerns about risk associated with the purchase

I will show you some of the useful closing methods to address these hesitations that the customer may have and thereby help him in his buying journey towards our product or service.

The following closing techniques are useful when the customer loves your product but doesn't feel the urgency.

a) The Urgency or FOMO Close

The Urgency Close or FOMO (fear of missing out) Closing technique is based on creating a sense of urgency in the customer's mind with respect to your product or service. The idea here is to **make the customer feel that taking immediate action is in their best interest**.

This approach nudges the customer into action because it taps into the psychology of scarcity and fear of missing out (FOMO). When a customer believes that a valuable opportunity is slipping away, they are more likely to act and grab the opportunity. This closing can help speed up the decision-making process and reduce the chances of a customer procrastinating or exploring other options.

However, it is important to note that while this approach helps to nudge the customer into taking action, it is generally effective when the product or service is either an impulse purchase item with no heavy price tag or if the customer has already seen many options and likes your product but is still contemplating or procrastinating in making the final move.

Let me take you through some examples of where this method works quite well with customers.

Customer: 'This bag looks great, to be honest, but I was planning to think it over. Can I let you know by tomorrow, and meanwhile, can you help reserve it for me?'

E-commerce Salesperson: 'This bag is the latest arrival for the season and is quite a popular item, and we have very limited stock for this. Unfortunately, I cannot reserve this item as it's a new arrival. My only concern is that I can see you like this product and by tomorrow it may be sold out. However, if you order today, I can also throw in a personalized tag with the bag, which usually costs around $50. But this offer ends at midnight.'

Customer: 'Alright, I'll place the order now in that case.'

Another example of how a travel agency salesperson uses this closing effectively.

Salesperson: 'This vacation package ticks all the requirements for your ideal vacation. And we currently have a double-digit day promotion running where, if you book now, you'll get a 20% discount and free pick and drop from the airport to the hotel.'

Customer: 'I agree, this package seems quite right for what I am looking for. But I was planning to book it next week.'

Salesperson: 'Of course, I understand, but the promotion ends tomorrow. Booking now will save you a significant amount of money, which you can then use during your vacation to delight your partner with shopping. What do you think?'

Customer: 'Okay, in that case, let's do it now and book the package for me.'

From these examples, you can see how a salesperson **can strategically use urgency to encourage customers** into taking immediate action. By highlighting the limited availability of the product or the time-sensitive discounts and special offers, the salesperson is able to create a compelling reason for the customer to decide promptly.

b) The Takeaway Close

The Takeaway Close approach involves withdrawing an offer or product temporarily from the customer, thereby creating a sense of losing the offer. This approach plays on the psychological fact that **when something is not available readily, people often desire that more**. When a customer is made to perceive that a product or service is now unavailable, they may reevaluate their decision and become more motivated to make a purchase to regain what they are losing, thereby getting them to act swiftly.

To illustrate this, consider the following instance of a salesperson helping a customer.

Salesperson: 'I'm sorry, but the red dress you liked is no longer available in your size. As I said, it is a popular design, hence it sold out quickly.'

Customer: 'That's disappointing! I really liked this dress.'

Salesperson: 'I fully understand. However, I do have a similar dress in blue that might still be available in your size. Shall I bring that?'

Customer: 'Yes, please! Let me try the blue one then.'

Real estate salespeople use this closing quite often to nudge their customers into action.

Salesperson: 'I have to apologize, but there's a strong interest in this property as being a corner unit, it includes access to a larger balcony. The seller informed me there is another buyer who is considering making an offer as we speak.'

Customer: 'I was really hoping to purchase this place.'

Salesperson: 'I can understand why; it's a fantastic property. Maybe I can speak to the seller and reserve it if you want to consider making your offer soon, before the other buyer does.'

Customer: 'Can you help me prepare an offer right away and block the property with a token down payment?'

c) Limited-Time Offer Close

Another closing technique to create urgency is using the Limited-Time Offer approach. This method creates a **sense of urgency in the customer's mind by placing a deadline on an offer or discount on the product or service.** It capitalizes on people's natural tendency to procrastinate on decisions until they feel they have a good reason to act immediately. So, when you present a limited-time offer to the customer, they often feel the urgency to act quickly to secure the benefits thereof.

To elucidate further, let's explore a practical application.

Salesperson (in electronics store): 'With this camera, I can put in an extra high zoom lens complimentary apart from the 20% discount that is currently running.'

Customer: 'It is good, but I need some time to think about it.'

Salesperson: 'I completely understand. However, this model has been very popular, and we've sold several today. The promotion ends tomorrow, so if you decide within the next 24 hours, I will still be able to retain the discounted price and the complimentary lens for you. But please bear in mind that this offer is applicable only to the stock we have left.'

Customer: 'Okay, in that case, I'll take it today.'

In a similar vein, this method can be used in online channels as well.

Salesperson (via chat): 'Hi! We can see that you have added two products to your online cart but have not yet checked out. We are now running a 20% discount on your cart items, but it's valid only for the next 24 hours.'

Customer: 'Yes, I know. I need to browse more options.'

Salesperson (via chat): 'Certainly, please take your time. However, I should mention that our 20% discount is a special promotion for the next 24 hours and the items in your cart are being browsed by many customers and have very limited stock. If you decide to check out now, you'll save on your entire purchase. You can even check out from our mobile app for your convenience.'

Customer: 'Okay, let me check out and complete the purchase.'

 Try the following closing techniques when handling customer hesitation regarding product, price, or both.

d) The Balance Sheet Close

The Balance Sheet Close is about showing the customer a **comparison between the cost or investment in your product or service and the long-term benefits and savings it can bring to the customer**. It is based on the concept of return on investment (ROI) to demonstrate that the advantages of using your product far outweigh the expenses.

This method helps provide the customer with a clear financial perspective that aligns with their desire to make sound financial choices and helps them visualize how the product or service will pay off over time. This helps the customer overcome their hesitations and makes it more compelling for them to make the purchase as now they can envision a profitable outcome.

Here is how this is effectively used, especially in the B2B sector.

Salesperson: 'Our digital marketing services will not only help boost your online presence but also increase your sales revenue. Based on my analysis of our existing clients in similar sectors, they've seen a 25% increase in website traffic within the first three months of using our services. Taking into account your current sales, this could mean an additional $50,000 in revenue annually.'

Customer: 'That sounds promising, but I'm concerned about the cost and investment in your solution.'

Salesperson: 'I hear your concern and can understand the hesitation. But let me break it down, and we take it from there. Our service costs $20,000 annually, but with an incremental sales revenue of $50,000, your net gain would still be $30,000. That's an impressive ROI achievement for the investment and worth it. Wouldn't you agree?'

Customer: 'Yes, indeed. Commercially, it does make sense.'

How can a salesperson selling high-end energy-efficient appliances use the Balance Sheet Close to help his customer?

Salesperson: 'Our energy-efficient refrigerator might have a higher initial price compared to standard ones, but they consume significantly less electricity. If you take your current usage into account, from my calculations you will be able to save at least $50 per month on your utility bills.'

Customer: 'I understand; however, I'm not sure about the higher upfront cost, to be honest.'

Salesperson: 'I understand your concern. However, our refrigerator is only $200 extra in comparison to other brands, but with at least $50 savings per month, this investment will balance itself in just four months and then it will be just plain savings. Additionally, over the entire lifespan of our product, you would save thousands. So, if you invest an extra $200 now in our appliance, you'd recoup that cost in just four months through energy savings. Over the appliance's lifetime, you will save thousands in the long run.'

Customer: 'Yes, that's convincing.'

Once you effectively demonstrate to the customer that their investment in your product or service will yield gains that far surpass the initial cost of investment in procuring your product, the customer feels compelled to see the purchase as a wise financial decision.

💡 When using balance sheet closing, it is always helpful to quantify the benefits to make an impact, and hence also the name Balance Sheet Close technique.

e) The Ben Franklin Close

The Ben Franklin Close is a very popular closing technique used by top salespeople. This **approach leverages the principle of cognitive dissonance, which suggests that when someone experiences conflicting thoughts, they get motivated to resolve them by acting.**

An effective way of using this technique is by encouraging the customer to actively participate in the decision-making process. While doing so, start listing the advantages and disadvantages or the pros and cons of your product or service, thereby making the customer realize that the benefits far outweigh any concerns. This also provides a structured framework to guide the customer to focus on the positives of your product or service and can help them overcome any pending hesitations they might have.

A key tip to remember here is: while you are doing this exercise, be proactive and write the pros for your products yourself (as you know best about your product or service), and when it comes to cons, ask the customer. This simple tip helps because, many times, the customers may not have many concerns or any at all, and when you ask for it, the customers themselves realize that their concerns may not be a lot and thereby become more accepting of your product offering.

Let's use an example of a car salesperson to demonstrate the effectiveness of the Ben Franklin close.

Salesperson: 'I understand you have some concerns about the car's price. Why don't we do a simple exercise? On this sheet of paper, let me write all the pros about the car on this side—it's fuel-efficient, has advanced safety features, an extended five-year warranty, and the perfect size for your family. On the other side, we can list any concerns that you have. What would you say are the most significant pros and cons for you?'

Customer: 'Well, fuel efficiency, warranty and safety features are definitely pros, but I'm worried about the price tag.'

Salesperson: 'Sure, let's write that down. Now, considering that with our flexible financing options, you can extend the payment period for over 24 months, which side do you think carries more weight in your decision-making?'

Customer: 'I suppose the pros definitely outweigh the cons.'

Salesperson: 'Exactly. This car aligns completely with your needs that you described before, and is a perfect addition to your family.'

f) The Contrast Option Close

Psychology says that **people perceive and appreciate differences more when they are highlighted in close succession.** This helps to create a clear contrast between the options, thereby making the preferred option more enticing. The Contrast Option Close is based on the same psychological principle.

As a salesperson, juxtapose the two options (including your preferred option for the customer) and create a clear contrast between them by highlighting the additional key value that your preferred option provides to the customer. By emphasizing the disparity between the options, the customer is more likely to focus on the differences and, more importantly, clearly understand the additional benefits that the preferred option provides, thereby making it easier for the customer to make the final decision.

A practical scenario where you can use this closing approach can be seen below.

Salesperson: 'We offer two versions of our software. The basic version covers essential features and comes at a cost of $50 per month. The advanced version, on the other hand, includes all essential features coupled with advanced analytics, 24/7 support, and lifetime software updates. The price difference between the options is only $15 per month. If you see both versions side by side, the advanced version not only allows you to access our entire suite of features but also includes dedicated customer support, all for a very reasonable extra fee.'

Customer: 'I was leaning towards the basic version, but now I see the value in the premium one, especially given the advantage of 24/7 customer support.'

Salesperson: 'Great choice. This is indeed the most subscribed version by our loyal customers too.'

In the same vein, very often you would have seen travel agents use the Contrast Close to make you purchase the preferred package.

Salesperson: 'Based on your requirements, I have two vacation packages for you. The first is our standard package, which includes accommodation, airport transfer and free breakfast. The second is our deluxe package, which includes everything in the standard package, plus exclusive guided tours, spa treatments and sports activities. The price difference between them is only $200. When you compare these two options, the deluxe package offers a once-in-a-lifetime experience for a minimal extra cost. If you book the add-on activities separately, they will easily cost upwards of $500 at the very minimum.'

Customer: 'The deluxe package seems to be worth it, now that I can compare them side by side. Please help me book the deluxe package then.'

g) The Anchoring Close

The Anchoring Close technique works by **strategically presenting a high initial price or premium option to the customer, which is called the anchor**. Any other subsequent offers then made by the salesperson will make them seem more reasonable and attractive to the customer.

The Anchoring Closing works because it influences the perception of value in the customer's mind. When you set an initially high anchor, it sets a reference point in the customer's mind and then any lower-priced option put in front of the customer automatically seems like a better deal and moves the customer into taking swift action, increasing your chances of closing the deal. Everyone likes a great deal and once you can make the customer realize they are getting a better deal, the decision-making process becomes much easier for the customer.

Let us take an example and see the Anchoring Close in action.

Salesperson: 'This smart LED TV has all the features you want and costs $5,000. However, we also have a slightly smaller model, which is also an LED Smart TV with almost the same features that you need, for just $3,000. It's a limited-time promotion and with this deal, you'll save $2,000.'

Customer: 'That's a fantastic offer. I'll take the $3,000 LED TV in that case.'

Salesperson: 'Excellent choice! Let me get it packed while I prepare the invoice for you.'

The Anchoring Close approach, when done correctly, lets the customer feel in control of the decision and that they are also getting a valuable product or service at a very reasonable price.

h) The Decoy Close

The Decoy Close method is, in some ways, **opposite to that of the Anchor Closing I mentioned above.** It leverages the principle that **introducing a less attractive but similar option (the 'decoy')** can influence customers to choose the more expensive or desired option. The difference here is that while the Anchor Close sets a high anchor point and then proceeds to mention the preferred options at a reasonable point below the anchor, in the Decoy Close, you set the reference low and unattractive and then showcase the preferred choice at a higher point and as more favourable than the decoy.

All customers love to evaluate options relative to other available options, and when you present the customer with a less appealing choice first, they often end up selecting the more expensive or favourable option, believing it offers better value in comparison to the first (decoy) option.

The decoy offer is very common, and I am sure you have seen this often around you, with the most common occurrence being in a coffee shop selling coffee in three cups of small, medium or large sizes. More often than not, the customer ends up buying the medium cup.

Let's see how salespeople selling service or products at a subscription model utilize this close successfully.

Salesperson: 'We offer three subscription plans for our video streaming service: a basic plan for $10, a premium plan with more features for $20 and a 'family' plan for $25, which allows up to four family members to use the same account with premium features.'

Customer: 'I think I will go for the family plan as it's only $5 more than the premium, and I can share it with my family members without having to pay for individual accounts.'

Another place where you often see this close being used is in gym memberships.

Salesperson: 'Our gym offers two membership plans: a silver plan for $50 a month and a diamond plan for $75, which gives you access to a trainer thrice a week along with access to a sauna and swimming pool. We also have a gold plan for $60 that's just right for most people as it gives access to a trainer thrice a week, which most beginners find more useful.'

Customer: 'The gold plan is only $10 more than the silver plan but gives almost the same benefits as the diamond option with access to a trainer, which is what I need the most at this point in my fitness journey. I think I will go with the gold plan for now.'

Salesperson: 'Excellent choice! Let me sign you up for the gold plan for now and whenever you feel you are ready to upgrade to the diamond plan, just let me know.'

 Closing techniques to handle customer hesitation and feeling risk in purchase.

Many times, the customer shows hesitation in moving forward with the purchase, which stems from the risk aversion that the customer has as he may be unsure about the credibility of the company or have doubts about the value proposition of the product or service. To help the customer, you need to share the positive experiences of other customers who have been satisfied with your product or service.

i) The Social Proof Close

The Social Proof Close is a powerful method used by salespeople to **leverage the positive experiences and feedback of satisfied customers to influence** potential customers. It relies on the principle that real-life testimonials and success stories from other customers can significantly influence the decision-making process of prospects.

The key advantage of using this method is that it helps build trust and credibility as it suggests that other people have already found value in your product or service, thereby reducing the perceived risk of making a wrong decision. Moreover, it leverages the human tendency to conform to the actions and opinions of a group, making it more likely for the customer to take a desired action and reinforce the value proposition of your product or service.

Here is an example of how a salesperson selling financial advisory services may use this close.

Salesperson: 'Mr Patel, I understand that you're looking for a financial advisor you can trust and who will work for your interests first. Let me share the success story of David, who, just like you, was seeking financial guidance. He chose our advisory services and, over time, achieved his financial goals of buying his dream home and also securing his children's financial future. We have many satisfied customers like David, and I am confident of making you our success story as well.'

Let us look at another application of this approach.

Salesperson (selling fitness membership): 'Sarah, I can imagine that committing to a gym membership can be a big step. But let me share a testimonial from Amy, who was in a similar situation. She had similar hesitations and reservations, but after joining our gym, she lost 20 pounds and gained a new sense of confidence. Her story is just one of many that highlight the positive impact this membership can have on your fitness dreams by turning them into reality.'

j) The Authority Close

This method of closing **leverages the idea that customers tend to trust and follow the guidance of credible experts or authorities in a particular field**. When your product or service is endorsed or recommended by a competent authority, it helps to reduce the scepticism in the minds of customers and also helps to increase your credibility as a salesperson.

This demonstration of expertise or authority helps instil confidence in the customer's decision to go ahead with the purchase. To provide further clarity and insight into this, consider the following example from the healthcare industry.

Customer: 'I see so many advertisements and claims by supplement companies, but in the end they do not provide any results. Hence, I have reservations about the claims of your health supplements.'

Salesperson: 'Jennifer, our supplements are formulated by a team of world-class nutritionists, and we have been featured in leading health magazines for their effectiveness. In fact, we are the only nutrition company whose supplements are FDA-approved and not just FDA-applied like others. Therefore, these are recommended by healthcare professionals. Our customers, including many elite athletes, have experienced significant improvements in their overall health and energy levels.'

k) The Storytelling Close

The Storytelling Close technique is a little harder to master as an approach, but once you get good at it, it is **a powerful approach to invoke emotions and engage the customer on a personal level**.

The strength of this approach lies in its simplicity. People love stories as stories capture attention and draw the customers in, making them active participants rather than passive listeners. Stories make the context of discussion more relatable and help evoke emotions, whether it is excitement, empathy or inspiration, and emotions are quite important in influencing the customer's decision-making process. People remember stories far better than facts or statistics. When this closing approach is used effectively, it helps to illustrate the value of your product or service much more effectively and helps build trust in the customer's mind.

The Storytelling Close is one of my favourites. Let me share an example of how using this approach, the sales team selling an online education service overachieved on their targets every time.

Salesperson: 'Hi, Mrs Kumar. I wanted to share the feedback about your son Sameer post his trial class with us. His trial class teacher was very impressed with his curiosity and the speed with which he grasped the concepts and applied them. She believes that Sameer has a natural inclination towards computers as it normally takes kids at least two to three classes to do what he accomplished during the trial class alone. So, congratulations on that! We would love to be a part of his journey and help him explore more in this field with our summer coding classes. Imagine when other kids are playing games on their phones, Sameer will be creating his own games through our coding classes. Coding is the language of the future, and we believe Sameer has all the potential to be the best at it. I am sure, as a parent, you would love to see this become a reality.'

Another example that emphasizes the effectiveness of this closing technique can be seen in the salesperson below selling smart home devices.

Salesperson: 'Mr Wick, imagine coming home after a long day at work, and as you approach your house, the lights in your house automatically turn on to welcome you. The thermostat has already adjusted to your preferred temperature, and your favourite music starts playing softly. We love to call this experience "a lifestyle upgrade". Our other customers who have installed our smart devices in their homes can't stop raving about how much easier and enjoyable their lives have become and how it has enhanced their quality of life at home.'

Effective storytelling helps to immerse the customer in a visualized experience with your product or service, thereby creating a strong connection in the customer's mind about satisfying their needs and desires. This makes the decision to purchase more appealing and desirable.

l) The Empathy Close

The Empathy Close is frequently used by top salespeople. It relies on the **premise of connecting with the customers**

on an emotional level by demonstrating understanding and compassion for their needs, concerns and challenges. Generally, when customers feel heard and listened to, they are more likely to trust the salesperson and be receptive to the solution being offered.

> One of the key differences I want to highlight between the Empathy Close and other testimonial-led closing approaches discussed above is that in the Empathy Close, the salesperson usually shares his personal story to empathize with the customer.

To provide better context, let me explain this with an example of a salesperson pitching career coaching services.

Customer: 'I see what you are saying, but I just do not know how to move forward.'

Salesperson: 'John, I sense that you're feeling stuck in your career and looking for guidance. It's a challenge I have seen many professionals face at some point in their careers. In fact, I was in the same place as you about five years ago, uncertain about my career path until I started working with a career coach, and everything changed for me. Today, I am happy to share that I am thriving and fulfilling my ambitions, and I would love for you to get that same support and guidance and shift gears in your career path. What do you say to changing gears for your career path now?'

Customer: 'Thanks, Ron. I think I will also give it a shot then. Let's do it.'

 Remember that for the Empathy Closing method to be effective, you have to have built a strong rapport and trust with the customer so that he believes you genuinely care about his or her well-being, not just making a sale.

Step 4: One Step Closer

We have reached step 4 of our closing framework, and this step is all about **being consistent, staying on top of the customer's mind, and helping the customer take baby steps in terms of commitment** towards your product or service. This step is all about how you can help the customer overcome the initial inertia of making the decision to take that leap. Remember, this is the penultimate step to reaching the pinnacle of MT CUSP and closing the deal.

There are a few proven closing approaches that I have seen work brilliantly in this step of the work and let me take you through them.

a) The Follow-Up Close

The Follow-Up Close, as the name suggests, is based on the idea that **consistent communication and attentiveness to the customer's needs** keep the engagement between you and the customer strong. It demonstrates commitment and a genuine interest in the customer's needs, which can then lead to a successful sale.

Moreover, frequent communication ensures that your product or service remains on top of the customer's mind and whenever they do decide, you can be sure to have your product or service in the strong consideration options.

 Important: One of the most common mistakes most salespeople make here is misunderstanding what follow-up means. It is not about sending unnecessary or non-relevant messages or simply broadcasting the same message to hundreds of customers and claiming follow-up. This is annoying. A proper follow-up is about showing your genuine interest in helping 'that' customer and not 'any customer'. It is about personalization in follow-up that makes the customer remember you. Broadcasting chats will make you end up on their block list forever.

One of the best salespersons that I have seen using this 'closing' is a dear friend of mine who is a top salesperson in the real estate industry. He always makes it a point to remember all his customer's wishlists and little nuances during their discussion, and during follow-up, he brings it up to the customer. Now, if you are that customer and the salesperson remembers and personalizes his follow-up with you, wouldn't you want to work with him only?

Let me share an instance when I saw my friend in action using the Follow-Up Close approach.

My Friend: 'Hi, Mr Kapoor. It's been a while since we last spoke about your home search. I wanted to check in and see if you are still looking for your dream home, as I've come across some new properties, and when I saw them, I thought of you instantly. I remember you prefer an east-facing house as per "vastu", and with a bigger parking space. I have three such properties that I know you will love. Would you be available to view them this Saturday?'

b) The Commitment Close

The Commitment Close is based on getting the customer to commit to the purchase of your product or service verbally or mentally before actually signing the deal. This method **encourages the customer to express their readiness to move forward in principle** with your product or service.

This type of closing method leverages the principle that once customers commit to a purchase notionally, they're more likely to follow through with it to align with their prior commitment. It leverages the psychological principle of consistency, where people tend to fulfil commitments they've made. Additionally, it reduces the buyer's remorse because they have already affirmed their intent to buy.

A salesperson can effectively use this method by asking relevant commitment-related questions and guiding the customer toward a positive response, making it more likely for the customer to close the sale.

Let us see how a fitness industry salesperson can utilize this approach when dealing with potential customers.

Salesperson (fitness industry): 'Sarah, considering your fitness goals and your current fitness levels, I recommend a minimum plan of three months to see optimum results. Are you comfortable committing to a three-month training programme to achieve your desired results?'

Or a real estate salesperson gently guides the customer into committing to the deal.

Salesperson (real estate): 'Mr Smith, I understand you have a few concerns about the property, especially with the lack of kitchen cabinets. However, considering all the other benefits and features it offers, if we redo the kitchen into a modular kitchen and address those concerns, are you ready to commit to making an offer?'

c) The Foot in the Door Close

The Foot in the Door (FITD) closing is about **getting the customer to agree to a small request, thereby making them more likely to agree to a larger one later**. Psychologically, people tend to behave in ways that are consistent with their past actions and commitments. Once they've said 'yes' to something small, they are more inclined and likely to say 'yes' to something larger to maintain that consistency, especially if that has worked well for them. This is called consistency bias, and this principle is at the heart of this closing approach.

This approach also puts the customer at ease since it allows them to test your product or service before moving to make a bigger commitment, thus reducing the risk for them.

This method of closing is one of the most successful and most utilized by salespeople across industries and geographies.

Someone selling a new software solution may face a lot of resistance in terms of product complexity, budget and, more importantly, alignment with clients' existing systems. Using this approach, you can help the customer be more at ease.

Customer: 'I can see from the demo and the features you have shown that your software definitely adds value, but I am a little hesitant as our internal systems are quite complex, and I do not know how well it will be able to perform for us.'

Salesperson: 'Tom, I understand where you are coming from and feel your hesitation. How about I set up a one-month free trial of our new software on a single team for the first month? It's an easy and low-risk way to experience its benefits firsthand. If all goes well, we can discuss rolling it out to the entire department. What does this sound like?'

Customer: 'Yes, this makes sense and if it works, it will be an easier internal sell to the other departments as well. Let us do this then.'

d) The Ownership (Perceived) Close

The Ownership Close works on the **simple premise that when people believe they own something, even temporarily, they are less likely to want to part with it**. This principle can be harnessed to encourage a purchase. If you can offer the customer a chance to experience your product for a weekend or a few days, more often than not, it becomes a part of their lifestyle and builds a sense of perceived ownership and emotional attachment to the product, which makes them more comfortable with simply purchasing it and keeping it.

This type of closing method is slightly different from the 'foot in the door' method as this generally works best with physical products with a significant price and impact on the customer's personal lifestyle.

Let me substantiate this with an example of a salesperson selling furniture.

Customer: 'I am 80% sure this sofa will look great with our house decor, but the price tag is making me want to be 100% sure before buying it.'

Salesperson: 'Mrs Belova, I understand that choosing the right furniture for your home is a significant decision. What if I arrange a trial period for this sofa? You can have it in your home for a week to see how it fits into your space and lifestyle. If you love it (which I'm sure you will), we can finalize the purchase. Sounds good?'

Customer: 'That sounds perfect if you can do it.'

Offering a customer a sense of ownership for the product allows them to experience the item or service firsthand and develop an emotional connection with the same. And once they've had a taste of ownership, there is a very big chance they will commit to the purchase.

> 💡 In fact, this technique is also used by many e-commerce companies today in the form of a free 30-day return policy or even providing a trial at your house and a no-obligation return if you do not like it. You would be surprised to learn that the average return is around 5–7% and 93–95% of customers end up buying the product. I would say that is a pretty good success rate.

Step 5: Go for It!

Congratulations, you have reached the pinnacle of MT CUSP. When you reach this stage, all your hard work has paid off, and you have won the customer's trust. Now, it is just about the paper formality, writing the terms and conditions, and signing the deal.

As you guide the customer through this final step, you need to be really careful and thorough. You want to make sure all the details are sorted out, and everyone is on the same page. It's like crossing the finish line, where you ask the customer to sign on the dotted line and make it official. You're basically crossing your t's and dotting your i's, making sure everything is clear and agreed upon. Plus, it's the start of a great partnership between the customer and you. So, don't underestimate the power of this moment—it's where success begins!

I hope that with this 5-step framework, you are now better equipped to understand in a logical way how to help your customers buy. Some customers are easy and some are tough, but with experience and consistent discipline, you will be able to handle most of them. The closing methods we discussed above will help you guide your thought process, but always remember to use them in the right context of your customer and their needs. Ultimately, it is all about the customer and helping him buy.

Now that you have climbed the pinnacle of MT CUSP, in the next chapter, I will tell you about how to get down (which, if you ask any experienced mountaineer, they will tell you is equally important) and how to make this a repetition of success.

After discussing various closing strategies, it's time to see how they perform in action. Reflect on your experiences, practise your skills, and plan your next moves with the upcoming assignments.

REFLECT

- From the 5-step framework of closing you learned in this chapter, reflect on the last few sales interactions and list down the step number at which you believed the interaction stalled or stopped. Now, write down the approach you followed against each of these stages.
- Taking the previous assignment forward and basis what you have learned in this chapter, write down how differently you could have handled the interactions and potentially have a successful outcome. Write down the revised approach or closing method that you think would have resonated better with the customer.

 **PRACTISE**

- Role-play and practise each of the five steps of the closing framework in different sales scenarios and record the outcomes. Ask your colleagues or friends to rate the effectiveness of the techniques you used and record them. Use this to identify which techniques are most effective with different customer profiles. This is, again, going to be a comprehensive assignment and very important.
- Now, from the list of techniques used by you in different stages and with different customer profiles, shortlist the ones that you are most comfortable with and the ones that go well with your style and personality.

 PLAN

- Integrate the list above, which is 'your personalized list' of closing techniques that work well and with effectiveness based on your personality and your customers, in your playbook under the last block of closing. Now, the first draft of your own personal pitch playbook is ready.
- Plan regular review sessions to assess the effectiveness of each block in your playbook. For a top salesperson, this playbook is a constant work-in-progress document and so should it be for you. It will help you to keep refining your approach based on outcomes, changing customer and market dynamics, and ensure that you stay ahead of the game.

10

Your Customer Service

'Top salespeople are great customer service professionals!' There is no bigger truth than this statement in the sales industry. Unfortunately, it is also the most overlooked and misunderstood concept when it comes to salespeople.

A lot of salespeople think their job is to make the customer buy and then move on to the next prospect and leave the customer handling part to customer support or after-sales support as their job is done. I cannot tell you how wrong they are in thinking and believing that. You did all the hard work in helping the customer buy, and now you have left them with the other team to provide support. This is a shortsighted mindset that can become the biggest bottleneck in your success.

Every successful salesperson will tell you it is **not just about climbing MT CUSP (closing the deal)** that has made them successful, but **rather their expertise in knowing how to climb down successfully (providing exceptional customer service)** and **repeating that over and over (referral customers)** again.

> Customer relationships are not one-time transactions, but rather ongoing partnerships.

Top salespeople know that their customer's buying journey is not a one-time buying experience but rather the start of a relationship which can convert these customers to potential advocates for their products or services. These potential advocates can refer new customers, provide testimonials, and contribute to a positive brand image, thereby making your job much easier with the next prospect. Therefore, maintaining a strong relationship with clients post-sales is of utmost importance.

For instance, a top real estate agent who has successfully closed a home sale knows the customer would need assistance with reliable movers and packers, maybe buying furniture (if they are new to the area), and nearby key resources. Connecting the customer with reliable movers or reputable contractors for renovations, or even offering advice on neighbourhood resources not only helps the customer and enhances the customer experience but also strengthens the trust in you as a salesperson. Needless to say, this increases the likelihood of future business opportunities and referrals.

> Think of customer lifetime value and not a one-time value.

A one-time sale is rarely as profitable as a long-term relationship. You can convert a single transaction into a series of sales over the years with the same customer simply by providing great customer support and excellent service. Keep in mind that customers are not static entities, and their needs evolve as time goes by. By being in touch with your customers and maintaining an open line of communication, you can anticipate the changing requirements of your customer and offer tailored solutions by upgrading them, upselling, or addition of new relevant products from your portfolio.

For instance, a salesperson in the automotive industry, after selling a vehicle, periodically checks in with the customer to enquire about any concerns or requirements. When the customer expresses a need for a larger vehicle due to a growing family, the salesperson is ready to provide suitable options. This proactive customer service not only highlights the salesperson's genuine commitment to customer happiness but also secures repeat business from the customer. After all, who would not want to deal with a salesperson like that?

Great customer service is a big differentiator today.

Top salespeople recognize that providing exceptional customer service in today's competitive market is an unparalleled differentiator. In a market where product and price parity are common and often compared, providing exceptional customer service becomes a vital competitive advantage. It helps nurture customer loyalty, which is oftentimes more valuable than acquiring new customers and also helps to retain your existing customers.

Sales triumph isn't about outsmarting the competition; it's about out-serving them with unparalleled customer care.

Let me share a personal example here. I travel often, but this one incident is still ingrained in my memory as a prime example of exceptional customer service.

Many years ago, during one of my trips, I was sick, and the moment I got onto the plane, I requested a glass of hot water to take my medicine and asked not to be disturbed by food service as I wanted to just rest. During the entire food service, I wasn't disturbed, and when I woke up after a few hours, to my surprise, the stewardess came to my seat with a dessert, saying she understood I was sick and did not want to eat but eating medicine on an empty stomach was going to make it worse. That care and concern for a passenger left a lasting impression on me, and I have shared this incident of unparalleled customer service many times. It is obvious this airline is still my preferred airline for flying and hasn't disappointed me until today.

> Objection handling is to sales AS
> complaints handling is to more sales.

Let's face it! Customer complaints are inevitable. Where rookie salespeople see complaints as something to be handled by the after-sales department, top salespeople see these as an opportunity to showcase their customer service skills. Recognizing the customer's time is valuable, they actively listen to their complaints, acknowledge the problem, and respond promptly to resolve it. This is what I call taking ownership of your customer.

Just like handling a customer's objections effectively can lead to a closing, similarly, handling a customer's post-purchase complaint promptly can lead to additional sales from them. Therefore, just like objection handling, complaints handling should also be viewed as a holistic part of a customer's post-purchase journey with you as their trusted sales partner.

Consider, for instance, a salesperson in the technology sector. If a client encounters a technical problem with the product or service, a top salesperson doesn't simply pass the issue to the support team. Instead, they take ownership of their customer's problem and work proactively to resolve it. This commitment to the customer not only salvages the customer relationship but also showcases the salesperson's dedication to their customer's success.

A good litmus test that I tell all the salespeople to determine how strongly the customer trusts them is by checking who is the first person the customer calls when they face a problem with the product or service. If the customer calls you to help them, you have passed the litmus test of exceptional customer service as, for the customer, you are the one-stop person for everything when it comes to your product or service, and this kind of trust by the customer is what top salespeople earn from their customers.

Now that we have understood 'why' providing exceptional customer service is important, let us move to the 'how' part of it, as a lot of salespeople think it is a time-consuming process, and they should rather be focusing on dealing with new customers. In reality, all it takes is 5–10 minutes of your time for each customer, and the returns on this little time investment are potentially huge.

So, how should you go about making customer service a part of your daily sales routine?

Schedule Timely Follow-Ups

Following up with customers after a purchase shows genuine care. This can involve a simple courtesy call, an email to ensure the product is working as expected, or sending a thank-you note. Such gestures make customers feel valued and appreciated. To do the same, make use of a scheduling software, calendar or mobile CRM app. This will help remind you periodically at predetermined intervals of time to reach out to your existing customers and have a quick follow-up. A simple gesture like this will always keep you at the top of the mind of the customer.

Always Provide Personalized Service

Though a follow-up helps to show the customer that you genuinely care and keeps you in the customer's mind, what solidifies this interaction for the customer is your ability to remember their preferences and needs. This personal touch can involve sending the relevant product recommendations by anticipating their needs, exclusive discounts, or even simple birthday or anniversary wishes. For instance, if your customer had purchased a camera from you, you might recommend a new lens that has been launched or even a photography workshop that you came across, thereby making the customer feel special.

Always Ask for Feedback

Top sales professionals actively seek feedback from their customers. Asking a customer for feedback on what else can be improved showcases your obsession with customer satisfaction and your drive to constantly enhance customer experience (a rare quality to find in salespeople today). This can help in identifying areas of improvement for your product or service or maybe even you. If you see a similar pattern in many customers' feedback, you know it is something to be improved upon.

Going the Extra Mile

Always be ready to go the extra mile for your customers. Even if it is not directly related to your product or service, going above and beyond in helping the customer never goes unnoticed and will earn the customer's loyalty and gratitude. For instance, let us say you helped a customer who wants to shed weight buy fitness equipment. During your follow-up call, they mention they are working out hard, yet the results are not of the same magnitude. Go the extra mile and help connect them to some nutritionists in your network or even share some educational resources like guides, webinars or articles that can help them achieve their goals.

To conclude this chapter, remember that your role as a salesperson doesn't end the minute you close the deal. You should be committed to delivering exceptional customer service throughout the customer's journey by focusing on post-sales care and building long-term relationships. **Nurturing this relationship will not only strengthen the customer's trust in you but also bring you referrals and repeat business.** This dedication to customer service is a hallmark of great salespeople, setting them apart and contributing significantly to their long-term success.

> Sales greatness is achieved not by chasing quotas but by exceeding expectations through exceptional customer service.

Having covered the fundamentals of impactful customer service, let's put these ideas into practice to see how they can improve customer satisfaction and loyalty.

 REFLECT

- Make a list of your customers and mention the last time you were in touch with them as part of customer service to check on their purchase or general follow-up.
- How would you rate your customer service on a scale of one to five once the deal is closed or even when the deal went cold?
- How does great customer service differentiate you from your competitors, considering the CARES approach from Chapter 1?

 PRACTISE

- In the list you made above, if the time interval in general catch-up with the customer is long or it is just missing (which is the case with most salespeople), then start today by populating that list with not just the customer details but also what they purchased, when they purchased, and any unique piece of information that you remember from the interaction with them. Take out 5–10 minutes daily and reach out to these customers for a courtesy checkup or follow-up. Use the unique piece of information that you recorded to personalize your follow-up customer service. This will always keep you at the top of the customer's mind and solidify your reputation as a trusted advisor instead of just a salesperson. Make this a recurring habit.
- Post every successful customer deal and even unsuccessful ones, reach out to the customer with a small feedback survey

requesting them to rate your interaction across the four to five areas of opening, product knowledge, understanding customer needs, objection handling and overall customer service. This will always keep you ahead of the competition; first, because generally salespeople do not do that, and second, the feedback from the customer (especially the ones who went cold) will greatly help you to refine your approach towards success. Remember: the best feedback is when the customer does not buy from you.

 PLAN

- The two sheets that you made above, one on customer service and the other on customer feedback, add them as part of your sales playbook. This will turn out to be one of your biggest assets as you keep using it.

11

Your Referrals

'Give a man a fish and you feed him for a day. Teach a man to fish and you feed him for a lifetime.' This old adage is very apt when it comes to sales as a profession.

Ask any salesperson to list down the challenges that are preventing them from clocking higher sales or making big commissions. Nine out of ten will rate the following two reasons in their list of top five challenges:

1. Limited number of leads
2. Poor quality of leads

At times, these reasons may be true but one thing I can say with conviction is you will never hear a top salesperson citing any of these reasons as their challenges. Why? Because top salespeople do not only rely on the leads generated by marketing campaigns or channels. In fact, for top salespeople, if you can ask them, over half their sales pipeline consists of prospects referred to by their customers.

In this chapter, I am going to teach you how to fish, and the fish I am referring to here is a **referral**.

Referrals in sales are a powerful tool that every salesperson should master if they want to make it big in their sales career. They are personal endorsements from satisfied customers who vouch for your product or service, thereby giving you a head start built on the foundation of credibility and trust when you handle new prospects. When a satisfied customer refers someone to you, it's an implicit endorsement that can be far more effective than traditional leads generated by marketing campaigns. People trust recommendations from those they know over advertisements.

Moreover, referral leads are often high-quality leads. And since they are coming to you based on a friend's or family member's recommendation, they are more likely to be genuinely interested in your product or service. These leads are pre-qualified by the referrer, who would have most likely already explained the value of the product or service and also your expertise in helping them.

Lastly, referrals allow you to acquire new customers without spending much. Except for referral incentives, you do not need to spend significant amounts of money on advertising or marketing to generate referral leads. In fact, many times, all you will spend is the cost of a phone call or email. And since referral leads have a higher propensity to be converted into successful sales, it adds to your increased sales as an added bonus.

Still not convinced? Let me share some convincing statistics for referrals.

- ***92% of consumers trust referrals*** from friends and family over other forms of advertising.[6]
- ***91% of Millennials would consider a purchase*** if it came recommended by a friend.[7]

---

[6]'Consumer Trust in Online, Social and Mobile Advertising Grows', *Nielsen*, April 2012, https://tinyurl.com/23rbey72. Accessed on 27 September 2024.
[7]'Winning Over Millennials with Referrals', *Annex Cloud*, 2017, https://tinyurl.com/47nsmr36. Accessed on 27 September 2024.

- **88% of B2B buyers say word of mouth** is the most influential factor in making purchase decisions.[8]
- **83% of customers are willing to refer** products and services.[9]
- B2B companies with **referral programmes are twice as likely** to have effective sales efforts than those without.[10]
- **Referrals are the most effective marketing** tactic according to B2B vendors.[11]
- Leads from referrals have a **30% higher conversion rate** than the leads generated from other marketing channels.[12]
- In terms of lifetime value, **referral leads are also ahead by 16%** compared to others.[13]
- Referred customers are **four times more likely to refer**

---

[8] Burger, Rachel, 'Why B2B Marketers Should Double Down on Referral Marketing', *Capterra*, 19 July 2016, https://tinyurl.com/4dwhca9c. Accessed on 27 September 2024.

[9] Chua, Desmond, 'Infographic: Why Referral Marketing is Awesome', *Referral Candy*, 1 December 2019, https://tinyurl.com/4bty5mnb. Accessed on 27 September 2024.

[10] 'Effect of B2B referral programs on sales and marketing in North America in 2015', *Statista*, 1 December 2015, https://tinyurl.com/5f6pn9uh. Accessed on 27 September 2024.

[11] Howarth, Josh, '22+ Referral Marketing Statistics', *Exploding Topics*, 14 November 2023, https://tinyurl.com/y927s833. Accessed on 27 September 2024.

[12] Ross, Lisa, 'The Importance of Referral Marketing – Statistics and Trends', *Invesp*, 21 September 2018, https://tinyurl.com/25ajjxnh. Accessed on 27 September 2024.

[13] Ibid.

your brand to others.[14]
- Referred customers have a **37% higher retention rate** compared to other customers gained through other marketing channels.[15]
- For every **one happy customer, you also get nine referrals**.[16]
- **82% of Gen Zers rely on their family's and friends' advice** when it comes to products.[17]
- **68% of Gen Zers are willing to recommend a product** they use regularly to a friend.[18]
- Meanwhile, **41% of Gen Zers will refer a friend just to qualify** for a reward.[19]

In fact, some of the top companies in the world also rely on referrals to build sustainable growth. There is a famous case of Dropbox, an online cloud storage company which I am sure many of you are aware of. From a mere 100k users in 2008, the company jumped to four million users by the end of 2010. Their success formula? Referral programme.

---

[14]Ross, Lisa, 'The Importance of Referral Marketing – Statistics and Trends', *Invesp*, 21 September 2018, https://tinyurl.com/25ajjxnh. Accessed on 27 September 2024.
[15]Ibid.
[16]Ong, Si Quan, 'The Ultimate Guide to Referral Marketing', *Oberlo*, 29 May 2022, https://tinyurl.com/mv7vjd4r. Accessed on 27 September 2024.
[17]Francis, Tracy, and Fernanda Hoefel, "True Gen': Generation Z and its implications for companies', *Mckinsey*, 12 November 2018, https://tinyurl.com/esnp52ns. Accessed on 27 September 2024.
[18]Ruff, Corinne, 'Price and rewards are crucial to Gen Zers and young millennials', *Retail Dive*, 26 February 2019, https://tinyurl.com/3y5tvv5s. Accessed on 27 September 2024.
[19]Ibid.

Dropbox initially started with traditional online marketing and soon realized their cost of new customer acquisition was coming to $230–$330 for a service being sold for $99 only. They realized this was not sustainable in the long run and instead tried using referrals as a means to acquire customers. Now, since they were paying the referred customers in storage space, it meant their referral plan was nearly free and way cheaper than paid customer marketing.

By 2020, Dropbox is sitting at 700 million registered users, out of which 15.48 million are paying customers. Their referral programme proved not only effective but also sustainable and continues to drive growth for them today.

I can quote many such success stories across many brands, but the point I am trying to drive home here is that even the biggest companies in the world with plenty of marketing budgets leverage referrals as their strongest growth driver for business, so why shouldn't you?

The Success Mantra for Referrals

The secret to cracking referrals and making them a staple addition to your sales pipeline is built upon two key pillars:

1. Exceptional customer service and experience
2. Reward for both referrer and referee

We have covered point one in detail in the previous chapter, and I hope you can now understand better why top salespeople are also top customer service professionals and the importance of providing exceptional customer service to your customers.

Point two is commonly referred to as a two-sided incentive, where both the referrer and the referee get some benefit upon successful completion of the transaction. In fact, it is quite common to have two-sided incentives built into referral programmes. It is estimated that 91.2% of referral programmes run by companies are double-sided. However, if your company falls into the other 8.8% or your company doesn't even have an incentive programme, DO NOT make it an excuse to not generate referral sales.[20] You can create your own custom referral incentive programme for your customers based on the potential deal value of the transaction and the amount to offer to both the referrer and the referee to claim your referral success.

Points one and two mentioned above are the pillars of a strong referral programme, but there is an overarching success mantra that you need to understand and embrace before you move to execute your referral pitch.

Referral is *Earned* and Not Simply *Given*

Every referral lead or prospect has to be **earned**. It has to be earned by providing exceptional customer service during and after the customer's buying journey with you. Without that, no amount of referral plan will work. Before you think you are ready to ask a customer for a referral, ask yourself these simple questions:

- What have I done for the customer that they should give me a referral?
- Have I earned the right to ask for a referral?

---

[20]'State of Referral Marketing Reward Structure 2020', *SaaSquatch*, 2020, https://tinyurl.com/48bbkxxw. Accessed on 27 September 2024.

Assuming you have 'earned' the right to ask for a referral, the next logical question is how you go about asking for it to the customer. Here are some proven methods for asking for referrals effectively.

How to actually go about asking for referrals?

Timing is Key

Always ask for referrals when your customer is the most satisfied. Typically, this will be either immediately after closing a successful deal, when they've praised your product or service, or when you have resolved a complaint or concern for them.

For example: 'I'm delighted to hear that you are happy with our product or service. If you know anyone else within your network or friend circle who could benefit from this, I'd be grateful for a referral.'

Be Direct and Specific

When asking for a referral, be direct and specific and not beat around the bush. Clearly express your request for referrals, as that makes it clear for the customer to act upon. You can say something like, 'Do you know anyone in your network who might be interested in our services and if you can kindly introduce me to them?'

Explain Your Incentive Plan

Always explain your incentive programme clearly and start by stating the benefits for the referrer first, followed by the benefits for the referee. Since most incentives are paid out upon successful transaction, stating the benefits for the referrer first makes the customer think of the people in their network who are most likely to purchase your product or service so they can get the incentive. Incentives also help to motivate your customers to actively refer you to others.

Leverage Your Network

If you are new to sales and do not have enough customers to ask for referrals, then reach out to your professional networks like LinkedIn. Send a personalized message to your contacts, explaining your request and why they might consider referring you to potential prospects in their network.

Host Referral Events

If you have the monetary capacity, then you can even organize events specifically aimed at generating referrals. Invite your customers for dinner and drinks and ask them to bring a friend who might be interested in your product or service. Project the event as an opportunity for customers to meet and network with like-minded individuals, so they are equally excited about turning up at the event.

Remember that when asking for referrals, it's very important to be respectful, professional and appreciative towards your customer. Always express your gratitude for any referrals you receive, regardless of whether they lead to a sale.

Referrals can significantly boost your sales. Use the following sections to deeply analyze, practise and perfect your approach to asking for and managing referrals.

 **REFLECT**

- Write down what percentage of your customers came from referrals of other customers, and what are the things you did that helped you 'earn' that referral from your customer?
- Map out your current referrals process, detailing out the steps and the effectiveness or percentage likelihood of obtaining successful referrals. (Leave it blank if you do not have a structured referral process.)

 **PRACTISE**

- Pull out the customer service sheet that you prepared in the last chapter and make a column for referral asked and referral earned. If you have earned the right to ask for referrals due to your customer service for the customer, this list is the starting point for asking for referrals. Top salespeople get up to 50% of new customers through referrals, so take this section seriously.
- Prepare a script or guideline for asking for referrals that includes personalization based on the customer's history with you. Remember, timing is key when asking for a referral. Practise the script with your colleagues or peers but with personalization to refine your approach to make it sound like a natural step in the conversation.

 PLAN

- Just as you make customer service a daily part of your process, in a similar vein, make asking for referrals (once earned) a priority as the referral leads convert 30% faster. Give it the same importance, if not more, that you will give

to handling new leads or customers. This here is the game changer, and I can't stress enough the importance of it. Make sure you are tracking it regularly and measuring its success in customer service/now also the referral list in your playbook.
- Develop a formal referral programme that includes clear guidelines and lucrative rewards for your customers and the referral customers. Incorporate feedback mechanisms to continuously improve the process. If the incentives are not lucrative for the customer, it will not incentivize them to refer.
- Practise different timings and approaches to asking for referrals, to see which yields better results for you with your customers.

12

Technology—Your Unfair Advantage

Technology has changed everything around us and changed the way we interact with people and things. Where technology has disrupted many industries and brought in new ways of getting things done, it would be unfair and incomplete if I didn't talk about how technology has penetrated the sales profession as well. Today, it has become a critical tool to not just bring about efficiency in our work but, more importantly, also to connect better with customers, who have all become tech-savvy.

Adapting to technology trends is of paramount importance for salespeople in the modern business landscape. I can give you several reasons why it is important to embrace technology, use it to your advantage, and stay ahead of the curve.

1. ***Matching Customer Expectations***: In today's digital age, most customers expect a seamless, tech-savvy experience for discovering their choice of products or services. They prefer to interact with sales professionals who can leverage technology and provide them with swift responses, personalized services and efficient solutions. Gone are the days of managing customer leads in a pocket diary. Today's customers are fast and fickle, and if we don't keep

up with their pace as salespeople, it will only result in lost opportunities.
2. ***Valuable Customer Insights***: With many available tools, such as CRM (Customer Relationship Management) software or analytics tools, you can gather and analyze your performance and pinpoint the gaps in your strategy while handling customers. These insights into customer behaviour, market trends and sales performance can enable you to make informed decisions and to tailor your approach to meet customer needs more efficiently. Salespeople who leverage this data can offer more targeted solutions, thereby increasing their sales.
3. ***Efficiency and Productivity***: Needless to say, one of the biggest advantages of technology has always been increasing efficiency and productivity across any industry. Using freely available tools, as a salesperson, you can reduce many manual and time-consuming tasks. You can automate data entry, email marketing, lead management and prioritization, and many more redundant tasks. You can then use this efficiency to focus on your core job, helping the customers in their buying journey with you. Use that extra time and energy to focus on making the customer's experience memorable. Use this increased productivity to close more deals and make more money.
4. ***Exploring the Global Market***: Digital platforms today allow you to tap into global markets. Using these platforms, you can advertise, sell and communicate with your prospects worldwide. This expands your market reach, making it easier to connect with new prospects and explore untapped opportunities.
5. ***Better and Swifter Communication***: Customers today

prefer to communicate across varied channels such as email, SMS, WhatsApp, Line, social media, video conferencing, etc. To ensure you are always available to help your customers across their preferred channels, you need to leverage technology to ensure effective and efficient communication. This will also allow you to provide faster responses to your prospects, which is particularly essential in a highly competitive market.

6. ***Competitive Advantage***: Sales professionals who are adept at using the latest tools can outperform competitors who are slower to adapt. There is no easy way to put this: adapt, embrace and evolve, or get left behind. Effectively using technology can provide you with that extra edge over your competitors. In today's competitive world, where everyone is fighting over the same customer, leveraging technology is not an option but a must for every salesperson to succeed.

With the advent of AI, a smart salesperson today can leverage it to make his job easier by automating repetitive tasks, streamlining workflows and gaining deeper insights into customer behaviour. There are tools available today that can handle lead generation, follow-ups and email outreach, thereby freeing up time for you to focus on high-value activities like closing deals. Using these tools, you can analyze customer interactions, predict which leads are more likely to convert, and formulate personalized sales strategies. Chatbots and virtual assistants can provide instant responses to customer inquiries, ensuring prompt service and a more engaging experience. With the help of these tools, you can work smarter, more efficiently and close deals faster, all while maintaining a high level of customer satisfaction.

Some of the essential tools that every salesperson should utilize can be grouped easily in the following categories:

- Lead Generation
- Lead Management and CRM
- Communication Tools
- Productivity Tools

Lead Generation

Top salespeople utilize various channels to prospect new customers to build their sales pipeline. Some of the tools that you can use for lead generation are:

a) Social Media: Leverage social media and networking platforms like LinkedIn, X and Facebook to connect with potential leads. Share relevant content, engage with comments, and send personalized connection requests. These platforms are also good for sharing your expertise with others, thereby engaging with people and gaining potential prospects for your product or service.

Did you know?

- 72% of salespeople who use social media in their sales process outperform their peers.[21]
- Social sellers hit their quotas 66% more often than those who don't use social media.[22]

---

[21] "Social Media and Sales Quota Attainment Survey", *A Sales Growth Company*, 21 September 2022, https://tinyurl.com/5n7r2u6c. Accessed on 27 September 2024.

[22] Morettini, Phil, 'B2B Social Selling and Marketing Strategy', *PJM Consult*, 2 March 2017, https://tinyurl.com/ms3kjza9. Accessed on 27 September 2024.

- 98% of sales reps who have at least 5,000 LinkedIn contacts consistently reach or surpass their sales quotas.[23]

To make your lives easier, there are various tools available today that can help you schedule and push your content to multiple platforms at once, so you can write once and publish on multiple platforms.

Some of the well-known software that I have used are:

  i. *HubSpot*: Offers comprehensive tools for publishing, monitoring and reporting on social media efforts. Its integration with HubSpot's CRM allows salespersons to track leads generated from social media directly in their sales pipeline.
  ii. *Hootsuite*: A popular choice if you have multiple social media accounts. It offers scheduling, analytics, content curation and team collaboration features.
  iii. *Sprout Social*: Provides a range of social media management tools, including publishing, analytics and engagement features. Its CRM capabilities allow for tracking interactions with leads and customers, making it easier for salespeople to follow up on potential opportunities.
  iv. *Zoho Social*: Offers scheduling, monitoring and analytics features, along with CRM integration. This makes it easier for salespeople to manage their social media activities and track leads in conjunction with Zoho's sales tools.

---

[23]Connaughton, Brendan, '135 Essential Sales Statistics You Need to Know in 2024', *Qwilr*, 26 February 2024, https://tinyurl.com/5e7mkvyj. Accessed on 27 September 2024.

    v. Buffer: A favourite with small teams and individuals for its clean interface and simplicity in scheduling posts across various platforms. It also offers analytics to track the performance of your content.

   vi. LinkedIn Sales Navigator: Specifically designed for sales professionals, LinkedIn Sales Navigator offers advanced search capabilities, personalized lead recommendations and insights to help salespersons find and connect with potential leads on LinkedIn.

b) Marketing Communication Automation: To reach out to multiple prospects at once, you can leverage tools that allow you to segment your prospect and customer list and automate sending personalized communication to them via email, SMS and instant messaging channels like WhatsApp. This kind of automation is very useful to nurture your leads and keep them engaged.

Some of the most used software that I would recommend you try and explore for yourself are:

     i. HubSpot Marketing Hub: It allows you to create personalized email and SMS marketing campaigns. It can also integrate with your CRM and track customer interactions across channels, enabling targeted outreach based on behaviour and preferences.

    ii. ActiveCampaign: Known for its advanced automation and segmentation capabilities, ActiveCampaign helps sales professionals send highly personalized emails and SMS messages.

   iii. Sendinblue: A versatile tool offering email marketing, SMS campaigns and chat. Allows for reaching out through multiple channels with personalized messages,

facilitated by its user-friendly automation workflows.
- ***iv. Twilio***: For salespeople who prioritize customizability, Twilio's API-driven approach to SMS, WhatsApp and email communications allows for the creation of bespoke outreach programmes that can scale customer interactions.

c) Content and Creative Development: Many times, to engage effectively with your customers, you will need to write content or make creatives for emails, blogs or personalized messages with a strong call to action, to use on social media. What used to require a dedicated team of designers and copywriters can now be done with a few clicks using generative AI software. Use it to create impressive content to reach out to your customers.

Try some of these tools below to see which one you feel most comfortable with.

- ***i. Canva***: Exceptionally user-friendly with a vast array of templates and design elements, making it the go-to tool for creating professional visuals without any design skills.
- ***ii. Mailchimp***: Offers a comprehensive suite for email marketing, landing pages and CRM functionalities, ideal for engaging with customers through personalized content.
- ***iii. Adobe Spark***: Easy-to-use design tools for creating graphics, web pages and videos, perfect for salespersons looking to quickly produce engaging content.
- ***iv. Buffer***: Simplifies social media management with scheduling and analytics tools, helping salespeople maintain consistent engagement with their audience.

v. ***ChatGPT***: ChatGPT can generate personalized content, emails and creative text for social media posts or any content for any sort of user communication. It's invaluable for salespeople needing to automate and personalize customer interactions without deep technical skills.

Lead Management and CRM

Lead generation is just one side of the coin. What is more important is how to effectively manage, prioritize and handle these leads or prospects and convert them into successful closings and higher sales. For this, I highly recommend investing and using a **customer relationship management (CRM)** solution to make sure your focus is on the right lead at the right time and you don't miss out on any opportunity.

CRM Software: Implement a Customer Relationship Management (CRM) system to manage and track your prospects efficiently. This system allows you to keep detailed records of your prospects and interactions, helping you correctly map where the user is in their buying journey.

An effective CRM system can also help you in keeping a strong structure and focus on each prospect with equal priority.

Using CRM, you can easily automate many routine tasks such as appointment scheduling, setting of reminders and even follow-up emails and other communication.

Additionally, you can even track the efficacy of the prospects and the channels through which you acquired them to determine the accurate return on your marketing and help you prioritize accordingly.

Did you know?

- 57% of sales pros spend 3–10+ hours per week using CRM tools.[24]
- CRMs can boost sales by 29% and productivity to 34%.[25]
- 24% more sales pros meet their annual quotas when they have mobile access to their CRM.[26]

Here are some of the CRM software that work well, whether you are an individual salesperson or a team:

a) ***HubSpot CRM*** is an excellent choice for individual salespeople due to its extensive free plan, which covers a wide range of CRM functionalities without overwhelming users with complexity. It's scalable and integrates well with HubSpot's suite of sales, marketing and service tools.

b) ***Zoho CRM*** is suitable for salespeople looking for an affordable, scalable solution with a comprehensive set of CRM tools. While user-friendly, it has a slight learning curve due to its extensive features. Free version is available for up to three users and has affordable premium plans.

c) ***Insightly CRM*** is a unique blend of CRM and project management tools, making it ideal for salespeople

---

[24]'The State of Sales Report 2021', *LinkedIn Sales Solution*, 2021, https://tinyurl.com/5329fsnd. Accessed on 30 September 2024.

[25]'18 Must-Know CRM Statistics', *Data Axle*, 13 December 2023, https://tinyurl.com/yk6u2shx. Accessed on 27 September 2024.

[26]Ostrow, Peter, 'CRM + Sales Enablement: Creating a Library of Success', *Aberdeen*, 18 August 2015, https://tinyurl.com/28nefyxw. Accessed on 27 September 2024.

who manage detailed projects with their clients. Its free plan is limited but provides essential CRM functionalities for small operations. Offers a free plan for two users.
d) **Freshworks CRM** stands out for its simplicity and powerful sales automation features. It's designed for salespeople who need an effective, straightforward CRM solution with advanced capabilities like AI-based lead scoring to prioritize prospects.

Communication Tools

a) **Video Conferencing Solutions:** With tools like **Zoom, Google Meet** or **Microsoft Teams**, you can hold virtual meetings with your prospects and make product demonstrations and presentations. In a remote world, these tools can help you engage with prospects regardless of their physical location, making the sales process more convenient and accessible.

b) **AI Chatbots for Customer Support:** Customers in today's digital age expect a quick and prompt response to their queries and concerns, and at times, this is not possible in person. However, using AI-driven chatbots, you can provide quick responses to customer concerns in real time and keep them engaged and keep them delighted.

Some of the popular and most used chatbot solutions are listed below.

   i. **Tidio** is ideal for salespeople who need a straightforward, no-fuss chatbot solution. Its drag-and-drop builder makes creating chatbots accessible, even for non-technical users. The free plan is generous, making it great for individuals or small teams.

ii. ***Drift*** is ideal for salespeople focused on B2B and looking for advanced chatbot functionalities, such as lead qualification and scheduling meetings. The investment is higher, but it's justified by the extensive features and potential ROI through improved lead generation.

iii. ***Chatfuel*** is a solid choice for salespeople targeting Facebook Messenger as their primary channel. It allows for quick setup of AI chatbots without needing to write code, and the platform guides you through the process.

Productivity Tools

a) Document and Proposal Management: Creating professional-looking documents like sales proposals, quotations or contracts is essential for every salesperson when dealing with customers. These tasks can often take up a lot of time and can be easily automated through the use of document and proposal management tools. They help streamline the creation, organization and distribution of documents and proposals within the sales process. Additionally, many of these software also offer integration with e-signature platforms, making it easy for clients to sign documents electronically.

These tools not only save time by automating the process but also improve the customer experience and increase the sales efficiency of a salesperson.

Check out the software listed below and give them a try.

i. ***PandaDoc*** is ideal for salespeople who need a comprehensive yet straightforward solution for managing proposals and documents. Its user-friendly design and robust feature set, including a wide range of templates and e-signature capabilities, make it a top choice for streamlining the proposal process. Also offers a free plan with basic features.

ii. ***Proposify*** offers specialized features for proposal management, making it suitable for salespeople looking to create compelling, detailed proposals. Its tracking and analytics capabilities are particularly useful for following up on sent proposals.

iii. ***DocuSign*** is an essential tool for salespeople prioritizing the signing process. It simplifies the completion of agreements with its leading e-signature technology and offers sufficient integration capabilities to streamline document workflows.

iv. ***Zoho Writer*** is an excellent option for salespeople on a tight budget needing a versatile document creation and management tool. It integrates well with Zoho CRM and other Zoho apps, facilitating an efficient sales process from proposal to close.

b) Calendar and Time Scheduler: Salespeople often struggle to manage their schedules and multitude of parallel tasks. These tools help the salesperson to improve their time utilization, task organization and coordination with prospects and clients. They allow the correct prioritization of crucial sales activities, thereby ensuring important meetings and follow-ups aren't overlooked or missed.

These tools can be leveraged to set priorities, allocate time to high-value activities, reduce scheduling conflicts and boost productivity for the salesperson, allowing them to focus on what matters most: helping the customer buy.

Here are some of the recommended tools that I suggest you use to make your day more structured and fruitful.

i. ***Calendly*** is perfect for salespeople looking for a hassle-free way to schedule meetings without the back-and-forth emails. It's simple to set up, and the free version offers enough functionality for individual users. Its ability to integrate with most calendars and offer time-zone conversions makes scheduling meetings with clients across the globe effortless.

ii. ***Google Calendar*** is an excellent choice for anyone with a Google account. It doesn't offer the automated scheduling features of dedicated scheduling apps but is incredibly effective for manually managing appointments and integrates well with other tools like Google Meet for video conferencing.

iii. ***Doodle*** simplifies the process of finding mutually agreeable meeting times by allowing you to create polls. It's particularly useful for coordinating meetings with multiple participants. The free version is quite functional, and the premium version adds valuable features for professional use if needed in the future.

iv. ***10to8*** is designed to make scheduling simple and reduce no-shows with automated reminders. The free plan is particularly attractive for individual salespeople or small teams, offering essential features to streamline the scheduling process and integrate with other business tools.

To close this chapter, I want to re-emphasize that adapting to technology is increasingly essential in today's dynamic customer-led environment. Sales professionals who embrace technology will be better positioned to thrive in this ever-changing sales landscape and come out successful.

Having delved into how technology can enhance your sales processes, proceed to the next sections to refine your tech strategies, and ensure they are effectively implemented in your daily operations.

REFLECT

- Map out your current process of handling customer data and needs. Where do you record it? Now next to it, list down all the challenges you face when dealing with your customers, which is preventing you from putting your best foot forward and offering each individual customer a tailored personalized approach.
- Prepare your wish list of tools that you would love to have to become an effective and smart assistant to you.

PRACTISE

- Take your list of challenges and the wish list you mentioned above and map them with the tools that are mentioned in the chapter.
- Now, experiment and test the tools and technologies that could fill the gaps identified in your reflection. Assess their impact on your sales effectiveness and efficiency. Some tools have a longer learning curve, so give it a proper try before giving up on it. Utilize videos on the product's website or even engage with their sales team to learn and assess the tool properly.

PLAN

- Develop and execute the technology adoption plan in a phase-wise manner (to avoid overload) that aligns with your sales goals, focusing on enhancing customer engagement, improving sales closure rates, and streamlining the sales process. Remember, technology has the potential to provide you with an unfair advantage over your competitors, but only if you are willing to work hard to adopt it and use it effectively. This is not the future anymore but the present.
- If you have a sales team, plan training sessions on the latest technology tools to ensure these are fully leveraged for sales success.

13

Parting Notes

'I will make it work' vs. 'let's see if it works!'—this mindset is the difference between a successful salesperson and an unsuccessful one. Like Thomas Edison famously said, 'Our greatest weakness lies in giving up. The most certain way to succeed is always to try just one more time.'

A lot of salespeople join with the hopes of making big money, but most of them quit within the first three months with a long list of reasons ranging from blaming the customer to the company, market, economy, and the list goes on. But the reality is that top salespeople will always find a way to make it work and succeed.

When I coach young salespeople, I always tell them one thing, 'I can coach you with the skills needed for sales, but I cannot teach you *character, passion and the will to succeed* as that is something within you, and only you can find it.' This determination and passion to succeed will always help you find a way to make it work.

Eleanor Roosevelt once said, 'Learn from the mistakes of others. You can't live long enough to make them yourself.' I have been a firm believer of this philosophy. There have been many great men who have tried, failed, made mistakes and laid the foundation of what works, and the smart thing is to learn from their mistakes and build on that foundation to chart your path to success.

I have always taken a keen interest in how some of the big brands have built brands or products with unparalleled customer loyalty. And after studying them for years and learning from them, I have come to one incontrovertible conclusion about their success—**Customer Obsession**. Anything that these brands have done has been built around the obsession to delight the customer, and the results are obvious.

So as a parting note, my first recommendation is to **be customer-obsessed**. Be obsessed with helping your customer so that you become synonymous with the product or service for your customer. Be obsessed with understanding their concerns and be obsessed with providing them with a memorable experience.

I agree that this is easier said than done, but then again, if it were that easy, then everyone would be a top salesperson. You will have your good days and bad days. Ask any successful salesperson, and they will tell you their success is built on the foundation of a lot of mistakes, hard work, frustration and rejection from their prospects. But they are committed to 'make it work' and turn around these 'no's' into 'yes's', and that is what separates them from the average salesperson.

With this book, I have tried to lay down the framework or structure to help you navigate, understand and ultimately help the customer buy. I have tried to keep it as practical as possible to help you get 'started and running' in sales as a career, but you will still need to practise, execute and retry many times till you figure out your individual blueprint for success.

This brings me to my second recommendation: **continue learning and evolving**. Every customer you will handle will teach you something new to add or update to your skill set. The day you think you know it all is the day you will stop growing in this career.

Sales is a rewarding career, with the only limit being the limitations you will set in your mind. So, become fearless and aim as high as you want. Remember, the higher the MT CUSP, the sweeter the reward and satisfaction will be.

To close the book, I will leave you with my final recommendation.

Treat every customer like he is your
ONLY CUSTOMER.

All the best and go for it!

Acknowledgements

No journey is ever undertaken alone, and this book is no exception. I am deeply grateful to all those who have contributed to its creation and made this project possible.

To my friends and colleagues—Mo, Hitesh, Nakul, Roland, Ayush, Saurabh, Jafar, Nicole, Katy and Vin—your camaraderie, support and thoughtful discussions have been invaluable throughout this journey. Thank you for your insights and encouragement, which have helped shape the ideas presented here.

A heartfelt thanks to my publishing team at Rupa Publications—Rudra and Sonali—for your tireless efforts in guiding me through the process. Your expertise and dedication have been instrumental in bringing this book to life.

To my mentors, Adrian and Mike, your wisdom, guidance, and the lessons you've imparted continue to influence my work in profound ways. I am forever grateful for your support.

To the thousands of customers I have had the privilege to serve and learn from throughout my journey as a salesperson—thank you. Your interactions, challenges and trust have been the foundation of my professional growth and this book.

Finally, to my readers, whose passion for knowledge fuels every word written here—thank you for your trust and time. It is because of you that this journey has been so rewarding.